EMBRACING UNCERTAINTY

Future Jazz,
That 13th Century Buddhist Monk,
and the Invention of Cultures

John Traphagan

EMBRACING UNCERTAINTY
Future Jazz, That 13th Century Monk,
and the Invention of Cultures
John Traphagan

Design by John Negru
Illustrations by Amane Kaneko

Published by
The Sumeru Press Inc.
PO Box 75, Manotick Main Post Office
Manotick, ON
Canada K4M 1A2

ISBN 978-1-896559-76-6

Publication of this book was made possible in part by
The Mitsubishi Heavy Industries Endowment Fund
at the University of Texas at Austin.

LIBRARY AND ARCHIVES CANADA CATALOGUING IN PUBLICATION

Title: Embracing uncertainty : future jazz, that 13th century
    Buddhist monk, and the invention of cultures / John W. Traphagan.
Names: Traphagan, John W., author.
Description: Includes bibliographical references.
Identifiers: Canadiana 20210227621 | ISBN 9781896559766 (softcover)
Subjects: LCSH: Uncertainty—Psychological aspects. | LCSH: Zen
    Buddhism—Psychology. | LCSH: Enlightenment (Zen Buddhism)
Classification: LCC BF463.U5 T73 2021 | DDC 158.1—dc23

 For more information about The Sumeru Press
visit us at sumeru-books.com

CONTENTS

For my father,
who has always inspired me
to think in new ways.

PREFACE

he ideas for this book have been percolating in my head for several years. The folder on my computer was created over five years ago, at which time the first six or seven pages were also written. From that point in time, it sat, unmolested, until 2021. As much as I want the pandemic to go away and sympathize with so many who have experienced the suffering it has caused, it has been something of a plus for me—and a constant reminder of the privileged position from which I am granted the opportunity to write and think. The commute from my kitchen to my study saves a great deal of time. And not having to devote attention to interminable administrative work and meaningless faculty meetings at the university also makes it much easier to concentrate on writing and thinking, which are pursuits I greatly enjoy. Writing provides a way for me to think through a problem. I usually write in a stream-of-consciousness mode, with no outline nor much of any plan. And that's one of the main points of the book—too much planning is not necessarily a good idea, because you never really know where you are going and if you plan too much, you miss a lot of experience and good thinking along the way. Writing is like that for me; I never really know where it's going. It just happens as I think through the interaction I experience with my computer.

But writing is also never an isolated act. There are all those people with whom I've shared thought-provoking conversations that influence the flow of my thinking. My father, Willis Traphagan, to whom this book is dedicated, has always been a key intellectual interlocutor for me. It's also from him, and my mother, that my love for music developed. Both of my parents were professional musicians, and our house was constantly filled with the sounds of mostly classical music when I was growing up. My immediate family—Sarah, Julian, and Tomoko—are always supportive and also help me think with spirited conversations, usually around the dinner table. There are also a few people who have been important in my ongoing intellectual development. Kelly Smith, a philosopher at Clemson University, is not only a good friend, but an intellectual force who routinely challenges me to reconsider my ideas. John Kaag, a philosopher at the University of Massachusetts Lowell, also has stimulated me to think in new ways not only through conversation but through his superb written work. An interview I conducted with University of California Berkeley computer scientist Edward Ashford Lee for my podcast on the New Books Network contributed to several of the ideas floating around in the pages that follow. Also, I greatly appreciate the support of my publisher, John Negru, who saw something of value in my work and decided to take it on for Sumeru Press. Many others have shaped my ideas, and I am appreciative of all with whom I have engaged over the years in ways that have changed my thinking and increased my uncertainty about what I think I know.

There are four people who I want to note as having been particularly important in my development as a thinker and as a person. Dean Bergeron, Joyce Denning, Nick Minton, and George Luter were professors in the history and political science departments at the University of Massachusetts Lowell when I was a student there. Joyce and George have passed on, but their words and ideas continue to shape my thought, as do those of Dean and Nick. It was in the classes of these dedicated teachers that my ability to think critically and to find ways to open my awareness to the ideas of others first truly emerged.

They were amazing guides who challenged every student who walked into the classroom to look at things with humility and sensitivity to the variegated nature of human experience. And it was these four professors who left me with a profound awareness that to be truly educated is to be forever uncertain.

Note: Normally, in academic writing, long vowel sounds in Japanese are written either using a macron over the vowel or with one of several possible spellings to indicate the long vowel sound. For example, the name Dogen has a long "o" sound, and is usually written as Dōgen, Dôgen, Dougen, and even sometimes Doogen, to indicate that the o is a long vowel sound. For the sake of simplicity, I have dispensed with this convention for this book.

Second

RIFFS AND LICKS

We seldom realize…that our most private thoughts and emotions are not actually our own. For we think in terms of languages and images which we did not invent, but which were given to us by our society.

— *Alan W. Watts*

’ve spent most of my life in the United States. I grew up in the Boston area and have lived on both coasts, the mid-west, finally settling in the southwest—in Texas. Fortunately, I have also had the opportunity to visit and live in many other countries, due to my work as an anthropologist and professor. The most prominent of these in terms of my experience is Japan, where my work has allowed me to live on and off for a total of about five years. Travel has a way of challenging preconceived ideas; living in another country can completely disrupt them. To experience the ways people in other places construct life is to be confronted with the fragility of convention and the capriciousness of normality. But one need not travel far in order to recognize this. One can encounter the diversity of human experience on the other side of town or by visiting a restaurant or bar where locals hang out. For me, moving to Texas was among the more disruptive cultural encounters I have experienced—I remember clearly when a student in class explained that there are Christians and Catholics, and they are not the same. Growing up in New England, I had never thought of religion in that bifurcated perspective, but came to learn over the years that it is by no means uncommon in the evangelical Bible Belt in the United States. Convictions held about polite and impolite, normal and abnormal, happiness and sadness, right and wrong abate if one's eyes are open to the mosaic of behaviors and ideas that humans use to navigate their world.

As a result of travel, the very notion that human experience can be carved up into binaries like normal and abnormal has come to make little sense to me. Through my visits to foreign and often alien places, I have concluded many of the challenges we face today are a product of thinking and living via the constant flow of binary oppositions between positions and ideas used by those in power, or those who want power, to simplify a world too complex to master. Love vs. hate. Guns vs. no guns. Masks vs. no masks. Pro-life vs. pro-choice. Religion vs. Science. Republican vs. Democrat. Good vs. evil. These binaries are inevitably intertwined with overt and covert political ideologies that draw from other binaries like Muslim vs. Jew, Catholic vs. Protestant, communism vs. capitalism, atheist vs. believer, which themselves are social categories constructed in part through a desire to achieve certainty and avert uncertainty, particularly in relation to perceptions about personal and social identity. So powerful is this binary way of seeing that we are prone to build reality itself in terms of juxtapositions between abstractions of nature and culture, the environment and the world of artifice, mind and body, chaos and order. Indeed, much of humanity is so wrapped up in constructing itself through simple oppositions that we find it difficult to think in any other way. Our society and our world seem immersed in a philosophy of life in which existence itself is experienced as a succession of simple dualities.

This is a book about imagining and living in a world not seen as an endless string of binary oppositions, but in a way that allows us to recognize the categories of past and future, right and wrong, emotion and rationality, human and deity, mind and body are cultural constructs—they are products of human imagination and creativity that, unfortunately, have constrained our ability to cope with suffering or build vibrant communities. The binary way of seeing the world is not something each of us harbors in our heads from birth; it is given to us, as Watts notes, by our society and shapes the way we think, but it is doing a great deal of damage to our social and natural environment as well as our psyches. Many of the problems we face stem from simplistic binary images we use to categorize the world—constructing the place in which we live as *having* an environment that is in some way opposed to the world our species creates; imagining that the religious ideas of our own peculiar group are unquestionably true, while those of others are unequivocally false; valuing our own society's way of life and devaluing the ways of life in other places, by, as theologian Martin Buber argues, objectifying others not only in ways that devalue them as humans, but that allow us to use them as tools to gain that which we desire (Buber & Smith, 2012). We live in a society and world that routinely orients itself around an evaluative trope drawing us to believe that life experienced at some imagined statistical mean expressed in our own beliefs is normal and good and all other forms of life are abnormal and bad, or at the very least of questionable value.

This book is a call to agnosticism. My interest here is to explore how we might live our lives built around an attitude that affirms the uncertainty of all claims to ultimate knowledge. I write from the perspective of an anthropologist who has spent several years living and studying in a society other than the one in which I was born and raised. My experiences in that place, as well as my readings and thinking about ideas drawn from Zen and Western philosophy, have led me to conclude that a worldview built around oppositions generates suffering. I'm not a Zen Buddhist and I make no claim to be enlightened—I'm not even sure what enlightenment is—although, as will become clear later in the book, I have some ideas. But I have come to see value in understanding the world in a way that recognizes the constantly changing and interpenetrating nature of Being revealed through the endless co-construction of reality in which humans and everything around them are constantly engaged.

In my thinking about the nature of reality, I've concluded that the culture of binaries humans often create misleads us into thinking about the world in terms of radical either/or images that typically are constructed as antagonistic oppositions. Connected to this is a notion of time as linear and a sense that "things" are always going somewhere as they move through this linear parade from past to future that so frequently ignores the present. I see both time and space not as a linear passage of events nor the comings and goings of things and beings, but as a constant rearrangement of all that is. Our world is like a kaleidoscope that, when turned, rearranges the parts to constantly create new designs, but the basic stuff of those designs is always there. And our lives are pieces in this kaleidoscope—we don't live in a march from birth to death, but instead experience an ongoing reshuffling of the stuff we are, including the physical aspects of our being and the memories contained in the physical matter that makes up our brains. Our birth is simply the emergence of a particular pattern of stuff; our death is nothing more than another reordering of that stuff. Throughout our lives, as we grow and age, the reordering never stops—it is an illusion that you are the same person you were five years ago or five minutes ago. Simply by reading these pages you have become something different and the "who" that is you has changed, while the "who" that was you no longer exists in quite the form it did only a few moments ago.

Human culture is also like this. Culture is a constant process of reordering social relations, and through that process novel arrangements—as well as reinterpretations of arrangements humans have already tried out—emerge as people improvise upon the values and rules created to hold them together in groups and ensure that some form of legitimate social order is maintained. Just as there are many individual ideas about the world, there are quite a variety of fascinatingly diverse ways in which humans organize themselves. I've long been intrigued by the different ways in which humans reckon family relationships. In the US, as in most Western societies, we view all our first cousins in the same way and, for the most part, avoid marriage between members of the generation who are related as first cousins. Not all societies work this way. The bifurcate merging system of kinship once practiced by Iroquoian societies of the northeastern part of North America but also found in South India, among Bantu speaking cultures of sub-Saraharan Africa, and in Melanesia, has an interesting way of thinking about siblings (Traphagan, 2008). For the Iroquoians, one's mother's sisters were all one's mothers while one's father's brothers were all fathers. This led to an interesting marriage arrangement in which it was possible to marry your cross-cousins, meaning your father's sister's kids and your mother's brother's kids, but not your parallel cousins. The reason for this is that because your uncles on your father's side and aunts on your mother's side were viewed as your parents, to marry their children would be to marry a sibling. That was viewed as incest.

There are several different ways in which humans have come to think about family structure—anthropologists call this kinship—including some that are focused largely on patrilineal descent and some on matrilineal descent. Japan, for example, emphasizes patrilineal descent and inheritance, but it is possible for an adult male to be adopted into his wife's line which, in effect, leads to matrilineality even while a patrilineal ideology is maintained—the adopted man takes his wife's name and assumes the position of eldest son in her natal household. The point to be taken away from this is that human family structures are, and long have been, complex, and there is no one correct way to think about kinship; and we continue to innovate new ways of thinking about kin relationships in the modern world as we improvise on the standard patterns of family formation in response to new ideas about what is or what can be normal. Gay marriage is a good example of innovation in the process of how people in several societies have come to think about what it is to form a family and who can be married; it is also a source of conflict between those who believe this change is for the better and those who choose to resist change.

The complex and changing cultures that humans constantly create through our interactions provide frames of experience through which we invent our world. As we move through those frames, many of the chance encounters and pivotal decisions in our lives turn out to be serendipitous. A great deal of the sense-making we employ to give meaning to our lives comes is the result of contextualizing our encounters and experiences, and in a sense re-inventing in the present in retrospect. This is often the case among musicians, who grow from interacting with others more than from formal educational experiences in theory and composition, for example. It is also that way with culture in general—we learn from experience as we co-construct our realities with others. As you move through the pages of this book, you will encounter stories that explore how I arrived at various perspectives and show the serendipitous nature of life.

A short walk from Takadanobaba Station in the Shinjuku section of Tokyo leads to a small sign pointing jazz lovers to the sub-basement in one of the area's tall buildings. After descending two flights of stairs, you reach the door of *Jazz Spot Intro*, a cramped and dark bar where local, and sometimes not-so-local, jazz musicians perform, often throughout the night. Chairs are tightly packed around small tables and the bar stretches into darkness at the back of the room. I've spent many evenings listening to tunes by Bobby Timmons or Thelonious Monk while wondering how the hell they got the baby grand piano down the stairs and through the door. In over thirty years of studying the culture, to me this remains one of Japan's greatest mysteries.

Until the pandemic hit, I regularly would hang out at *Intro* on summer Sunday evenings for open mic night. Most of June and July was time I spent teaching courses on Japanese culture at nearby Waseda University to international students. The jam sessions gave me an opportunity to play—I'm a drummer—and keep my chops in shape until I returned to Austin and my regular jazz trio gigs. There were always some exceptionally skilled musicians at *Intro*; and usually some who were only beginning their journeys into the world of improvisational performance and mastery of an instrument. But the environment was supportive and open to anyone willing to put themselves and their musical abilities on public display.

On one evening, my turn had come to sit behind the drum set. As a newcomer and infrequent participant, my opportunities at *Intro* are limited—I usually only get to perform two or three tunes before they move on to another drummer who has a more established presence at the club. This also means that I typically perform with a mix of experienced and beginning musicians. A woman who appeared to be around 50 years old also came on stage and let the group know she wanted to sing *Autumn Leaves*, a jazz standard from the 1940s performed by jazz and pop music greats such as Frank Sinatra, Sarah Vaughan, Johnny Mercer, and even Iggy Pop. I was pleased—*Autumn Leaves* is one of my favorite tunes because there is an elegant simplicity to the chord structure and melody that opens the door to unlimited improvisational possibilities. The singer gave us her tempo and we started. As the pianist and bass player read the tune off their music, they followed the chords laid out in the key of E minor. Unfortunately, the singer had different ideas and started in an undefined key that clearly was not E minor. Being the drummer in our make-shift quartet, there was little I could do beyond cringing and trying to keep a steady beat while watching my stage mates on piano and bass as they looked at the charts and held back mild panic amidst consideration of whether to transpose into the singer's key. We stayed in E minor, which turned out to be a good unvoiced collective decision, because the singer cycled through several other keys, none of which were E minor, before we reached the instrumental solos. Those solos turned out to be quite a bit of fun, and we managed to get some good musical conversation going, particularly when the drums and piano traded fours. Eventually, it was time for the singer to rejoin, which brought relieved smiles to our faces—she had found E minor!

Jazz performance has a great deal in common with cultural performance. Life for humans is basically an ongoing process of improvisation around a set of vaguely pre-established forms that we call culture. The social or cultural context in which we are born and raised provides a set of structures or rules that guide the way we grow into adulthood and navigate our interactions with others. Language is central in this—we learn a language and treat the structures of that language as normal. That is, until we start learning a different language and realize that what we thought was normal is just one take on the many ways communicative events can be organized. I'll come back to this later.

One of the common misunderstandings about jazz is that when musicians improvise, they simply make things up on stage with other musicians. This is not at all what is happening in a jazz performance. Improvisational jazz is structured and usually predictable if one is socialized into the forms and tropes that characterize the music. Jazz musicians don't read music the way classical musicians do—instead of all the notes being written out, they work from a rough form called a lead sheet that provides a general map consisting of the chord structure or "changes" and the melody. The melody is written out on the staff and the names for the chords, such as C seventh (C7) are placed above the notes in the melody at the point where they are expected to change, often at the beginning of a new bar, but also routinely within a bar as the melody progresses. Figure 1 is an example of how this looks on a typical lead sheet.

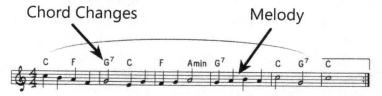

Figure 1, Example of a lead sheet.

Jazz standards, which are commonly played by most jazz musicians, include tunes like *I Got Rhythm* or *The Man I Love* and follow a common form known as AABA, which is a 32-bar structure divided into eight-bar phrases. The A section establishes the initial melody and is repeated, following which there is a B section or "bridge" that takes the melody in a different direction that contrasts with the A section. The circle is concluded with a return to the A section to complete the overall song-structure. Other forms, like ABAC, exist, but the AABA pattern is by far the most common in jazz. And because jazz musicians know this form, they can predict how most tunes will unfold in a performance, even if they've never previously played the tune. This also allows them to perform together and improvise even if they have never met. Several times after a set, I've had people in the room come up and ask, "how long have you guys been playing together?" suggesting that our trio is musically well synchronized. We are, but this will happen when we have a substitute on one of the instruments, such as bass. When we reply, "oh, about 45 minutes now," we get astonished looks. But it isn't astonishing; as long as we select tunes that follow a basic structure or for which we have lead sheets, the pattern is so predictable that we won't usually have problems. On occasion, something may come up, such as an extra bar inserted in a pattern that might throw us a little, but this is unusual. The main issue that arises is on occasion our bass player and pianist have different lead sheets and don't realize it until they start—in different keys. But that can be fixed on the fly.

Not all jazz musicians make regular use of lead sheets. It's essential for those who play melodic instruments like the piano unless they've memorized the music being performed, but as a drummer I generally don't bother with a lead sheet unless I'm playing a tune I've never encountered. The lead sheet gives me the form and is important if a tune is following an atypical structure. Bass players often use a simplified form of the lead sheet that only has the changes—no melody. It looks like this:

Cmin7/F7/B♭maj7/E♭maj7/Amin7(♭5)/D7/Gmin7/G7

That is the A section for *Autumn Leaves*. From this information, a bass player will understand the changes for the tune and be able to "walk" a bass line to support the melodic instruments such as piano or trumpet. For the most part, like drummers, bass players are not engaged in performing the melodic parts of a tune; they provide rhythmical and harmonic foundations for the melodies that are played by other instrumentalists or singers. A good bass player or drummer, however, will find a way to build the melody into her performance, particularly in the context of solos, as she interprets the changes. Great players, like Jaco Pastorius (bass) or Joe Morello (drums), find ways to develop alternate interpretations of the melody not only in their solos, but also throughout the performance of a piece, often as counterpoint to the ideas of the person soloing.

When a jazz group like a trio begins to play *Autumn Leaves*, the first time through they usually play it "straight" meaning they follow the changes and melody in a conventional way. There is still improvisation in this, because the ways in which the performers interpret the lead sheet varies. For example, unlike most other instruments, the piano involves playing the chords (guitar is also like this). But there are multiple ways to play the same basic chord. A C major chord is conventionally written as having the notes C, E and G, but this can be played in any order with E at the bottom, C at the bottom or G at the bottom. Thus, E/G/C, C/E/G, or G/C/E. The way in which a pianist decides to do this is called voicing and voicings create a particular sound that in some cases, such as the great jazz pianist Bill Evans, are immediately recognizable to the seasoned listener. Evan's voicings are so distinctive that one can quickly recognize his recordings—or in some cases the performance of someone who has channeled Evan's music, like one jazz pianist I've performed with in Japan. With my eyes shut, I wouldn't be able to tell the difference. As they say, mimicry is flattery and much of what we learn in a given culture, or in musical performance, is the result of mimesis (the embodied reconstitution in our own patterns of behavior of the things others do in theirs).

When playing the tune straight, jazz musicians also often create novel interpretations of the tune, adjusting the values of the notes and creating different feels. If you listen to the way saxophonists Charlie Parker and Dexter Gordon play *Autumn Leaves* it will sound different. The tune will be immediately recognizable, but there will be subtle differences in phrasing and feel, as well as in the tones they produce through their instruments. The fun comes during the solos, which is the context in which the most innovative improvisation is usually done, but there remains a very structured aspect to what happens. The overall form, like AABA, is normally followed and each musician will go through that form several times as they develop their musical ideas. Those ideas are expressed via the paths that the musicians take with the melody—and even the changes—to head in novel directions that arise in the context of the performance as they interact with each other. A great jazz performance involves pushing the melody and changes in inventive ways that surprise both the audience and the other musicians (who will find interesting responses to what others in the group present). For a simple example, when the pianist in my trio plays an interesting rhythmical form during his solo, I may pick that up and echo it on the snare or bass drum. If the musicians are technically able and know the music well, a conversation will often emerge as they collectively improvise off the melody and changes and with great musicians even the basic form itself. This conversational aspect of jazz is readily seen in what is called trading fours (or trading twos, eights, etc.). During the solos, and often involving the drummer, musicians will sometimes alternate four-bar (it can also be two or eight bar) phrases in which they exchange ideas, often echoing back patterns played in the previous four-bar frame. This trading represents a conversation involving musical ideas and can become quite fascinating as the musicians listen to and musically comment on each other's ideas.

However, even within this conversation there are patterns and conventions. Jazz musicians learn riffs, or brief musical phrases that are memorized and become part of the overall lexicon that a musician uses in improvisation. As I wrote that, pianist Oscar Peterson was playing in the background and I heard one of his typical riffs—which I am likely to hear in most of his performances. Jazz musicians learn to string together riffs, repeated chord progressions, as an anchor to the improvisational patterns that they create in a performance. They also learn licks, which are repeated single-note melodic lines used in the context of improvisation. The familiarity of riffs and licks allows one to avoid getting lost while in the process of improvisation and provides technically manageable patterns that are easy to remember and play while trying out new musical ideas. Jazz musicians don't just create riffs and licks; they also learn riffs and licks created by other musicians as a way to develop their musical knowledge and skill. And they will employ what they learn in their own solos as a way of quoting the ideas of other musicians.

There is very little in the way of binary opposition in a great jazz performance. Instead, when a group of musicians begins improvising around the changes and melody in *Autumn Leaves*, improvisation becomes a collective and humble practice of merging with the musical context by listening and responding to the ideas of others in the group. Skillful musicians (in any genre) listen to each other and build their own interpretations of the music they are playing collectively. This can be quite powerful. When a trio is having a great night, the musicians may lose a sense of individual self-identity as they perform. One becomes so completely absorbed that one *forgets oneself.* Humans have understood this experience for centuries and it doesn't only occur in music. About 800 years ago, the Japanese philosopher monk Dogen Zenji described it as *opening oneself.* As far as I know, he wasn't a musician, but forgetting oneself and opening oneself are essentially the same thing. In forgetting oneself, one becomes open to the possibilities, ideas, and emotions expressed by others and by one's surroundings and allows all that is around to penetrate one's sense of self in an undifferentiated way.

Returning to my rough night at *Jazz Spot Intro*, when our singer entered in a different key, the entire communicative and improvisational context was disrupted. This meant that improvisation was largely impossible because the underlying form had been broken. The other musicians on stage resorted to a simplified structure for their playing—the pianist just tried to hit the chords, the bass player walked the bass line, and I tried to keep time—in a fraught attempt to hold everything together until we got to the solos. What emerged was a binary in which the singer and the instrumentalists were following somewhat opposed pathways through the musical performance. More experienced musicians might well have been able to follow the singer on her journey through the circle of fifths, but our group was just trying to stay afloat. Once we reached the solos, the form was re-established, the binary dissolved, and we were able to improvise freely around the melody and changes provided by *Autumn Leaves.*

If you were to replace the words *jazz* and *music* with *culture* in the above description, I think you would have a very good understanding of how culture works in human groups. From my perspective, culture is the lead sheet that provides a form and set of expected patterns from which individuals and groups often collectively improvise social interaction and life itself. Each of us read that lead sheet in different ways on the basis of our role in the group—things like occupation, position of leadership, expertise—and the personal experiences we bring to our encounters. Interactions with others involve licks and riffs—a good example is "Good morning! How are you today?" And we routinely improvise off those licks and riffs as we encounter others using their own versions of commonly held patterns. If I say, "how goes it?" there is a good chance that you understand the proper response to be something like "fine, and you?" We both know that neither of us really want an answer to that question, and when someone answers, "terrible, my car broke down this morning, my dog ran away, and I got fired" there is a good chance that it was not the conventional and expected answer. This can be good or bad, depending on who is listening. Failure to use the "fine, and you?" lick will lead to a minor breakdown in the structure or a polarization, similar to what I described at *Jazz Spot Intro*, but it is easily repaired by a response like "I'm sorry to hear that" followed by an attempt to quickly extract oneself from the conversation. But this depends on the interlocutor. If the person at the other end is a friend, then a long conversation or improvisational interlude in the normal flow of life may develop around that bad day and its consequences. It depends on context and who is listening.

Jazz is the same way. If the musician takes things too far away from expected improvisational tropes, the music becomes either annoying or difficult to understand and the listener may move away. I find this to be the case with the free jazz developed by saxophonist Ornette Coleman and others. On the surface, it sounds like everyone is just doing what they want and there is no structure; in fact, it's quite difficult to find the structure, but if one listens carefully there are riffs, licks, and changes that are expressed and followed. However, for me, these are not melodic and harmonic approaches I want to hear when listening to jazz (just like I probably don't want to really know how you are if I ask), so I don't listen to free jazz very often. I do, however, think Coleman was a brilliant musician because he pushed the boundaries of what we think of as music through a radical approach to improvisation that questions the nature of form and structure within the jazz genre. He intentionally created a kind of binary through challenging current jazz convention as a way of generating innovative musical ideas and, as a result, he manipulated the concept of jazz to expand our understanding of the genre.

There are Ornette Colemans that do the same thing in the course of social interactions beyond the confines of artistic performance. One of them is Donald Trump. Trump excelled in generating a disruptive discourse and he appears to have done this largely off the cuff while following an underlying lead sheet that frames the basic parameters of his improvisational behaviors. If authorities indicate mask-wearing is essential, then argue the pandemic is a hoax. If the media notes inconsistencies or lies in his speeches, then it's fake news. I don't need to give many examples here to show that Trump has been successful engaging in a radical improvisational approach that questions the form and structure of American society and its government. He was so successful that his words helped to stimulate an insurrection using riffs and licks, the conventional tropes of Trumpism, like "the fake news and the Big tech" or "we will stop the steal" to guide his improvisations—both of these riffs are quotations from his Insurrection Speech.

If the lead sheet charting out the melody and changes for the insurrection of 6 January 2021—in this case the ideological patterns and tropes of the radical right wing—were not already there, Trump's words would make little sense to any segment of the public. The strategy Trump employs is intended to polarize—to take advantage of the tendency of humans to see the world in terms of binaries by creating simple us/them oppositions that disrupt feelings of social integration and collective responsibility and, therefore, allow people to dehumanize those with whom they disagree. Although Coleman was not trying to dehumanize those who saw jazz in a conventional way, the strategy he used in his album *Free Jazz: A Collective Improvisation* has commonalities with the Trump strategy. The album represents the cornerstone of the free jazz movement, an experimental approach to jazz improvisation that emerged in the late 1950s and through which musicians attempted to challenge jazz conventions related to things like harmonic voicing, changes, and tempos. Some musicians of the time felt restricted in their ability to pursue their own musical-improvisational interests within the conventions of forms like bebop and hard bop, not entirely unlike the feelings of restrictions people at both ends of the political spectrum tend to feel about the conditions of their social and economic lives.

In terms of the general public's reaction, Trump was far more successful than Coleman in creating disruption, although Coleman's aims were less to change the musical proclivities of a popular audience than to challenge his fellow musicians to think in new ways. Like Trumpism, free jazz is only partially something new. It draws on early styles of collective improvisation that existed in jazz prior to the swing era, but also innovated American musical patterns with use of instruments from other parts of the world such as Asia. Free jazz was not the only locus in which this challenge occurred, even if it was among the most controversial. The Dave Brubeck Quartet challenged jazz convention with its much less overtly radical album *Time Out*, on which they performed *Take Five*, which is among the most recognizable jazz tunes ever written. *Take Five*, performed in the time signature of 5/4, meaning five beats per measure, was a departure from conventional jazz forms of the 1950s that were usually in four or occasionally three beat time signatures. Most of the tunes on the album experiment with different time signatures, such as *Blue Rondo à la Turk*, which is in nine, although the solo section of the tune is in four, which provided a familiar foundation to the rest of the tune. *Time Out* reached number two on the Billboard pop album charts, selling over a million copies—clearly somebody liked it, despite its counter-conventional nature.

The subversive qualities of *Time Out* are covert, as opposed to the overt radicalism of Coleman's *Free Jazz* album. Although *Time Out* had some critics among the jazz community, who thought it was too attuned to the mainstream of popular culture, in general the reaction was positive perhaps because the tonal and harmonic qualities of the tunes on the album all stay firmly anchored within conventional jazz forms. *Free Jazz* generated more polarized responses among jazz critics; Pete Welding gave the record five stars and John A. Tynan gave it no stars. Welding wrote, "It does not break with jazz tradition; rather it restores to currency an element that has been absent in most jazz since the onset of the swing orchestra—spontaneous group improvisation. Yet Coleman has restored it with a vengeance; here we have better than half an hour's worth, with only a minimal amount of it predetermined to any degree." Tynan had a somewhat different perspective: "The only semblance of collectivity lies in the fact that these eight nihilists were collected together in one studio at one time with one common cause: to destroy the music that gave them birth."[1]

Brubeck's *Time Out* was in its own sweet way just as unconventional as Coleman's album, but the unconventionality in the use of time signatures was expressed in standard harmonic forms and visually presented through conventional licks and riffs like the dark suits, white shirts, and narrow ties that the group wore, and which appealed to a white middle and upper-class audience. And despite the unusual time signatures, the basic structures of the tunes follow typical jazz patterns as I outlined above—in fact, the solo section in *Blue Rondo* is a standard blues form in four. While the album broke

---

1   http://www.thejazzrecord.com/records/2015/9/15/ornette-coleman-free-jazz

conventions of jazz meter, it also in some ways broke social conventions such as becoming the first jazz album to sell a million copies and its lack of jazz standards—every tune on the album is original, which meant that listeners didn't have the well-known tunes like *Autumn Leaves* to ground their listening. But the group was already widely popular among socialites and intellectuals—they had made a living touring college campuses in the 1950s—so people were ready to take a chance with a familiar jazz group's crossing into a musical subversion that has some parallels to the much less subtle subversion of social norms generated when white jazz pianist Dave Brubeck made headlines in 1960 after cancelling a twenty-five-date tour of colleges and universities across the American South after twenty-two schools refused to allow his black bassist, Eugene Wright, to perform.[2]

When I think about the response to Coleman's *Free Jazz,* I find it interesting that it came in binaries. Critics tended to love or hate it; and writers like Welding and Tynan built their arguments around ideas that there is an authentic or true form of jazz. For Welding, true jazz is what he perceives as the original approach of collective improvisation and, hence, he sees the album as "restorative" of an authentic jazz music. Tynon, in contrast, represents the album as destructive and an affront to jazz itself and he even attacks the musicians when he describes them as nihilists, a word that has also been used to describe some of Trump's more enraged followers.[3] Indeed, the response to Coleman is quite similar to how people have seen Trump—he is either a defender of American values or an affront to those values. It's a binary. And that binary is a response to the radical challenge these men directed at conventional tropes—the riffs and licks of the objects they attacked—as they improvised.

---

2   Kelsey A. K. Klotz, "Dave Brubeck's Southern Strategy," *Daedalus,* Spring 2019, https://www.amacad.org/publication/dave-brubecks-southern-strategy.

3   https://theconversation.com/dostoevsky-warned-of-the-strain-of-nihilism-that-infects-donald-trump-and-his-movement-152807

In comparing these two men's approaches, I want to be clear that I'm not comparing them as people. Coleman was a musical genius (I know nothing of his personal behaviors); Trump is among the most disgusting presences I've encountered in my sixty years on this planet. However, I want to raise the idea that both individuals used a disruptive form of improvisation to challenge convention and conventional expectations about the worlds of jazz music and politics in which they operated. And that approach generated uncertainty leading to a binary response through which their ideas were viewed as unambiguously right or wrong. The problem with this is that such responses, particularly when they are on the critical extreme of the binary, usually fail to grasp the underlying logic of the approach taken by those who engaged in the subversion.

In Coleman's case, many of the basic structures and patterns of jazz are there if one listens carefully—it only sounds cacophonous if you can't hear the logical structure of the music. In fact, although the album consists of over thirty minutes of continuous freeform improvisation there are two brief, pre-determined sections that anchor the work. It is by no means chaotic, but the structure is very difficult to grasp if one either isn't deeply socialized into jazz forms or doesn't want to follow Coleman in his diversion away from those forms. It requires deep listening. *Free Jazz* is not background music for an elevator.

Trumpism, like free jazz, builds on pre-existing forms and ideas. It is a product of the far-right wing of the Republican Party with its evangelical roots and racist/sexist philosophy of disdain for anyone who conceives of life outside of that religio-fascist bubble as desirable and normal. If you read Sarah Ruth Hammond's book *God's Businessmen: Entrepreneurial Evangelicals in Depression and War*, I suspect you will quickly find that the common riffs and licks Trump and the GOP right wing use, in performing their take on American society, as well as societies outside of the US, go back at least to the 19th Century. I'm not interested in exploring the ideology behind Trump's performances over the course of his presidency—that is best left to political scientists. To me what is interesting about Trump, like Coleman and many others, is that they engaged in disruptive practices that challenged convention. The response to this challenge is typically that people group into binary positions in which they see the "other" as wrong and themselves as right. In fact, I see this as a broad tendency in American society—and in many other societies. There is a need among a significant portion of the population to be right which can only be confirmed if others are unambiguously wrong in their behaviors and beliefs. Being right allows for security and is often grounded in an imagined past, whether yesterday or 100 years ago, when things were done properly.

We live in a society based on the quest for security and that security is frequently built upon simple, binary images drawn from a past constructed by those with whom we agree or at least come to think we want to agree. Unfortunately, the craving for security is like a feedback loop—the more we desire security through simplistic quests for certainty, the more we suffer in the often covert awareness that real security cannot be achieved. In other words, the attempt to achieve security is a self-reinforcing quest to find certainty. It is to be increasingly right while others with whom we disagree are increasingly wrong. This might be okay if we lived in a world that doesn't change. But our world is one of constant change. We can try to run from that change and hide in the comfortable confines of certitude and righteous confidence about what we believe to be true. But that will only generate more suffering when we become confronted with realities of change such as loss, disagreement, and disappointment. Claiming certainty is a hedge against the uncertainty we continually face in life because we have no way of knowing what will come next in our ever-changing world. The consequence of this is that if we really want to deal with the uncertainty that permeates our lives, rather than resisting it by situating ourselves in binary frames that juxtapose unambiguous positions of right and wrong, good and evil, nature and artifice, believer and atheist, communist and capitalist, we need to embrace uncertainty as a mode of being in the world.

As will become clear thought the rest of this book, by embracing uncertainty I am not claiming we must walk a middle path in which we forever sit quietly on the fence, refusing to take a firm position about what we believe. My interest in agnosticism is not intended to present a message encouraging passivity or non-engagement with the world in which we live. Rather, to embrace uncertainty is something that can be generated by what I view as the ethnographic outlook. As I mentioned earlier, living in other places has a way of disrupting one's own assumptions—one's sense of certainty—about the way people live and should behave. It challenges our notions of normality and can be profoundly humbling. To embrace uncertainty is to live by the idea that those things I take for granted as normal are normal because the culture in which I happened to be born has provided a set of parameters through which people construct the identities and behaviors of themselves and others, as well as their collective identities and behaviors. in terms of an authentic, unchanging reality. The ethnographic perspective is one in which we remain open to other ways of seeing that might undermine our own sense of what is right and wrong and question our preconceived notions about the world. In short, it means being open to being wrong, or at least to the possibility that there may be more than one way to be right.

2

THE ETHNOGRAPHIC OUTLOOK

To practice zazen automatically, unconsciously and naturally
is to look at oneself.

— *Taisen Deshimaru*

everal times over the course of my career, I've been asked by my students how it was that I came to be an anthropologist who studies Japanese culture and society. What generated my fascination with Japan? What goals did I set early in life that allowed me to achieve the lofty position of professor at a major research university? They always hate the answer. The road to becoming a professor of anthropology was not a smooth one for me, nor was it linear. I majored in political science as an undergraduate and then started an MA degree at Northeastern University in the same field. To say that I majored in political science is something of a misnomer. That is what's on my transcript, but in truth I focused on political philosophy. I took as many classes as I could in that area, which I augmented with courses in international relations. At Northeastern, my advisor kept encouraging me to focus on public administration, because that's where the jobs were. But I didn't want to do that.

Fortunately, a friend of mine was studying at Yale Divinity School and he prodded me to apply. Somehow, I was admitted, promptly resigned from Northeastern, and prepared to move to New Haven to study for an MA in Religion focused on social ethics. That topic seemed a lot closer to political philosophy than public administration. If I'm honest about my past, I really have no idea why I applied to and attended Yale, other than it seemed like it would be cool to study at Yale and at least I could spend my time reading and thinking about something that interested me. I went with the flow and it turned out to be a good decision. Yale changed my life, but I certainly did not plan for that and I had not set any goal to attend an Ivy League school for graduate work. It just sort of happened (which illustrates my earlier point that pivotal moments in our lives can be unscripted).

While I was at Yale, I met two professors who challenged me to think in new ways. One of them was at the Divinity School—a guy named Tim Jackson, who was a newly minted PhD from Yale and went on to an accomplished career as an ethicist at Emory University. The other was a physicist named Henry Margenau. Henry took me under his wing as something of a final project in his career, which had involved research and publication not only in physics but also philosophy. He was among the prominent philosophers of science of his generation, as well as an important scientist working on the theory of microwaves as applied to transmission with radar. We spent many hours in his office discussing not only his own writing on the nature of the physical world, but also the philosophically oriented works of other physicists like Werner Heisenberg and Erwin Schrödinger, who had become interested in ideas like those expressed in eastern mysticism. I'm pretty sure we dissected Fritjof Capra's *The Tao of Physics*, a book with problems not only in the presentation of physics but also in the presentation of eastern philosophical concepts.

Henry had an abiding interest in ethics and its potential relationship to scientific reason and even wrote a book that explored the relationship between ethics and science (Margenau, 1964). Despite our significant age difference—Henry was in his

80s when I met him in my 20s—we became good friends and stayed in touch until he died. Somewhere during my conversations with both Margenau and Jackson, I realized that I was fascinated with understanding why people do what other people tell them to do and a related question of how we construct reality rather than simply submitting to the forces of an external world, and these questions led me to pursue a PhD in religious ethics. This linkage between political science, philosophy of science, and religious studies continues to interest me today.

I enrolled at the University of Virginia, which at the time had one of the top programs in religious ethics in the US, so I was delighted to have been admitted. I lasted one semester. The problem was that at Yale, I had become quite absorbed in the writings of a philosopher named Richard Rorty. Rorty's work fits within the philosophical confines of American pragmatism and his most important book, *Philosophy and the Mirror of Nature*, aims to undermine the idea of knowledge as representation and the belief that our minds somehow mirror the external world (Rorty, 1980). Rorty's thinking centers around a challenge to the belief that reality is independent of both mind and language and that people like anthropologists, physicists, ethicists, theologians, and philosophers build their understandings of truth upon an objective reality independent of human cognitive activity. In other words, Rorty's philosophical project is a provocation intended to undermine the notion of binary opposition between mind and world and replace that with a kind of moral middle way in which the subject/object binary is rejected in favor of a concept of truth as communal representation of how people wish things to be; thus, our ethical practices are the products of collective human creativity rather than a reflection in our minds of an external objective reality.

Although I spent hours in the library at Yale Divinity School reading and re-reading *Philosophy and the Mirror of Nature*, it was a brief article Jackson assigned in our seminar on skepticism entitled "Postmodernist Bourgeois Liberalism," which Rorty published in the *Journal of Philosophy*, that thoroughly disrupted my thinking and, ultimately, ended my budding career as a religious ethicist. Rorty's stated goal in the article is to argue against some human need for a foundational morality seemingly external to our society or our existence as *homo sapiens*. He states that for a collective of people—a society:

> ...loyalty to itself is morality enough, and... such loyalty no longer needs an ahistorical back-up...The crucial move in this reinterpretation is to think of the moral self, the embodiment of rationality, not as...somebody who can distinguish her self from her talents and interests and views about the good, but as a network of beliefs, desires, and emotions with nothing behind it— no substrate behind the attributes. For purposes of moral and political deliberation and conversation, *a person just is that network*, as for purposes of ballistics she is a point-mass, or for purposes of chemistry a linkage of molecules. She is a network that is constantly reweaving itself...not by reference to general criteria (e.g., "rules of meaning" or "moral principles") but in the hit-or-miss way in which cells readjust themselves to meet the pressures of the environment (Rorty, 1983). [emphasis added]

In other words, the moral self is not a reflection of some ideal about right and wrong evident in an objective reality, but an ongoing construction *within* the context of social and cultural value sets—the rules of meaning—that are themselves constantly being reinterpreted and which humans use to cope with their social and physical environments. A person does not *have* a network of beliefs, ideas, ideologies, emotions and so on. A person *is* that network. To be human is to be a social construct that experiences life through interaction with other social constructs and, therefore, is constantly changing in relation to the improvised and ongoing social interactions within the boundaries of conventional values. In hindsight, it's clear that this passage set me on the path to becoming an anthropologist, although I had no idea that's where it would lead at the time. It also moved me to explore the area of moral relativism, or the sense that we have no objective basis upon which to determine that one community's way of doing things is any more or less right than another's. At the end of the article, Rorty responds to the claim that his argument leads to relativism and argues that his post-modernist perspective is not intended as relativistic, but because we are trapped in the flow of history, we have no choice other than to build moral systems that recognize our ideas about right and wrong, as is all knowledge, are inherently embedded within the contexts from which they emerge. Therefore, everything we think we know is *contingent* on social and historical context; and because social and historical contexts are always changing, knowledge of the true or of right and wrong is constantly changing, as well.

This brought me to the writings of Duke philosopher David Wong, whose work centers on moral difference and the extent to which we find similarities and contrasts across different societies. The thesis of Wong's book, *Moral Relativity*, is simple—there exists no single true morality. Morality, for Wong (1984), is a product of "critical reflection on the adequacy of moral systems" that we use to regulate conflicts of interest among people and that are important elements in how we construct personal desires, needs, and goals. In other words, to ask what is moral is to ask about the extent to which the moral systems we create meet our needs at a given time and place. The problem of the existence of a true morality, then, must be understood in relation to the question of whether the idea of what an adequate moral system might be varies in terms of social, historical, and temporal contexts.

Both Rorty and Wong argue that morality is a product of human imagination expressed through culture, which means there are different versions of right and wrong and those things change over time, even within a particular social and cultural context. A good example of this can be found in the history of jazz. The genre has its roots in the blues and ragtime music of the late 19th and early 20th Centuries and developed significantly in New Orleans' Storyville, a Red Light district that provided the only venues in which African American performers could develop their musical ideas, due to their being banned from white clubs. The growth in popularity of jazz in the 1920s was accompanied by campaigns to censor the "devil's music" and some detractors, such as Thomas Edison, made snide comments that the musical form sounded better played backwards. There was even an instance in Cincinnati in which a home for expectant mothers successfully pursued a court injunction to prevent construction of a theater where jazz would be played, on the grounds that the music would be dangerous to the unborn fetuses. Many communities in the US enacted laws to prohibit the performance of jazz in public.[4]

Think about how different jazz is today. Where I live, it's associated with clubs that cater to hipsters and wealthy clientele who seek an evening of sophisticated entertainment, or at least that atmosphere. Intellectual elites travel to New York City to spend several days hopping from one jazz club to the next, and Jazz Studies are among the possible majors at prestigious music schools like Julliard or Eastman. In other words, a musical genre that was at one time constructed in large part through tropes of American racism as morally depraved has come to be viewed over the past century as a locus of high art. No doubt, a significant part of the reason for this was the entrance of white musicians into the jazz scene in the 1930s, such as Artie Shaw with his highly popular big band, which for the dominant white culture legitimized the jazz genre. And, of course, the racist construction of jazz as morally deviant has been directed at other forms of African American musical invention such as rap (Gay, 2000).

---

4   https://www.pbs.org/wgbh/cultureshock/flashpoints/music/jazz.html, accessed 24 April 2021.

This example points to the fact that morality is not an objective "thing" we find somewhere out there in the universe after which we can model the inner workings of our individual minds. It is something created by humans embedded in the flow of cultural and historical discourse. This realization presents serious problems for a moral viewpoint dependent on justification of ethical tropes on anything external to human creativity—whether it be natural law, divine command, or something else—because it means humans are *responsible* for determining what is right and wrong and that determination will change as our knowledge changes over time. There is simply no way to be certain about what behavior is morally true beyond an analysis of how a given culture builds a rational framework through which to make moral judgments.

My advisor at Virginia, as far as I could tell, didn't much care for Rorty's pragmatist philosophy and probably had similar feelings about Wong's moral relativism, because the notion of ethics being contingent and basically a human invention made it rather difficult to pursue a principle-driven biomedical ethics career (his area of specialization) based on what he viewed as a universal common morality that all moral beings intuitively understand and follow. We had a few conversations about this in his office, although he rarely had a great deal of time to talk with graduate students, and during one of those conversations I voiced a growing interest with learning about ethics in Japan. He looked me in the eye and said, "don't waste your time on that; they don't have an ethical system in Japan."

At the time, the comment seemed unlikely, and I wondered how an entire society of humans could somehow function without an ethical system. Today, when I look back at that moment, I simply see the comment as incredibly ignorant and ethnocentric. Of course, Japanese people have an ethical system. But in one sense, he was right, because that ethical system doesn't operate in any way like the principle-based concept of ethics to which my advisor adhered. Instead, it is a lot closer to what Rorty and Wong describe—it's a system based on the idea that right and wrong are situational and context-dependent. They are contingent, and any determination of right and wrong is inevitably going to involve uncertainty and ambiguity. In fact, it is precisely that understanding which leads to the powerful emphasis on being humble and self-effacing that permeates Japanese culture.

I lasted one semester at Virginia. Between my disagreements with my advisor and my agreements with Rorty, it became clear that ethics was not going to be my thing after all. Discouraged, I returned to my parents' home in Massachusetts and hunted for a job. The only skill I had was writing, so I looked for work in that field, which I managed to find quickly, largely on the prestige value associated with my Yale degree rather than my skill as a writer. And over the next few years, I worked in technical writing and editing at software companies, the most important of which was Digital Equipment Corporation. The job wasn't important, but it happened to be the place where I met my future wife and it was she who one day uttered a simple comment that completely changed my direction, yet again. As we ate dinner one evening, she said, "you are wasted in the business world."

It wasn't long before I was applying to PhD programs, still in religious studies, but this time I decided to focus on Buddhism. I had no idea what I was doing. In fact, I was rather naïve about the extent to which language study was going to be involved in becoming an expert in Buddhism—typically it means learning Japanese, Chinese, Classical Japanese, Classical Chinese, Sanskrit, French, and German. Ugh. Most of the programs to which I applied rejected me, perhaps in large part because I lacked any of the language skill, other than German and one year of Japanese, needed to complete a PhD in a reasonable amount of time. But the University of Pittsburgh had a new assistant professor joining the faculty who was a specialist in East Asian Buddhism and they also needed a research assistant to work as the managing editor for the *Journal of Ritual Studies*. I'm sure that it was my editing/writing background that got me admitted to the program rather than my interest in Buddhism—it certainly wasn't my preparation to study religion in Japan.

Pitt proved to be the perfect place for me to become a scholar. But the religious studies department again left me feeling like I had headed down the wrong path. Fortunately, in my first semester I took a graduate seminar on religion and culture with an anthropologist named Keith Brown. In one of those incredibly odd twists of fate, it turned out that he had spent years doing fieldwork in the very town in which my wife had gone to high school in Japan, although she was not familiar with him. In fact, he did his first long-term fieldwork in that town in 1961, the year I was born. My encounter with Keith turned out to be another turning point, because as I read for his seminar and discussed culture and Japan with him in his office, I realized that although anthropologists did not spend a great deal of time thinking about ethics (in those days, they do more now), their perspective on human culture had a great deal in common with Rorty's and Wong's ideas about morality.

In the seminar, we read an article by the eminent anthropologist Cilfford Geertz (rhymes with hertz) called "Ritual and Social Change: A Javanese Example." Geertz's goal was to show that there was a bias in the social sciences, and particularly anthropology, toward showing societies as well-balanced and integrated systems that functioned to keep people organized and unified. This approach went back at least to the work of sociologist Émile Durkheim, who viewed structures like religion as the cultural glue that hold people together in social groups, which is done by setting up contrasts of self and other in which self is associated with the moral and good. Although it didn't occur to me at the time, Geertz was dealing with the same binary mirroring problem and its relationship to social change that had intrigued Rorty. Geertz wrote:

> One of the major reasons for the inability of functional theory to cope with change lies in its

> failure to treat sociological and cultural process-
> es on equal terms; almost inevitably one of the
> two is either ignored or is sacrificed to become
> but a simple reflex, a "mirror image," of the oth-
> er. Either culture is regarded as wholly deriva-
> tive from the forms of social organization...or
> the forms of social organization are regarded as
> behavioral embodiments of cultural patterns...
> (Geertz, 1957)

Geertz uses the ethnographic description of a funeral in Java that fails to operate as expected to get his point across. The normal process of ritual grieving in the village he studied ends up being disrupted due to an "incongruity between the cultural framework of meaning and the patterning of social interaction," which occurred when religious symbol systems associated with agricultural social structures became inter-twined and ultimately in conflict with urban administrative systems. The moment of social discontinuity Geertz described arose when a ritual leader arrived to begin the funeral cere-mony after the death of a villager. He saw a political symbol associated with a religion other than Islam and, since he didn't know the correct burial rituals of that religion, indicated he was afraid he might insult the other religion by making a mistake in performing the rituals. The family of the deceased was taken aback because they lacked a sense of this type of exclusivity in ritual performance. The result was that a representative from the family had to go to the local police and village head's of-fice to get forms signed so that they could move forward with preparations of the body for burial.

Geertz showed through this article how the meanings as-sociated with symbols change over time, including religious and administrative symbols, and that the process of change is generative of disruption when institutional and other struc-tures—such as recently arrived religious institutions, govern-mental organizations, or changing patterns of residence—find themselves in conflict and resist contrasting ways of managing a social, political, or cultural problem. Geertz's description and analysis is nuanced, and a powerful sense of the idea that culture is a process, rather than a thing, emerges from the work. There is also a message that people construct their ideas of normality in terms of imagined authenticities that can at times come into direct conflict, creating disruption in the conventional flow of cultural performance.

I liked Geertz a lot when I was in graduate school and I still do, despite the fact that several scholars have argued that his approach to ethnographic analysis has problems. Of course, every scholar's work has problems because we can't know everything, but more importantly scholarship itself is always changing. Our knowledge about other cultures as well as our methods for learning about other cultures is just as contingent as our knowledge about ethics.

After one semester, I transferred to the anthropology department at Pitt. As you read this, you may notice a trend in the one-semester riff I repeatedly played during my graduate education. There were several reasons for performing this particular manifestation of the riff at Pitt, not the least of which was the fact that I had no desire to learn all those languages. Modern Japanese was difficult enough. In anthropology, I could develop a good study on some aspect of religion or ethics in Japan without having to devote years to learning languages that were of absolutely no interest to me. But there was a more important reason. In anthropology, I had found an intellectual home that didn't simply tolerate contingency—it embraced it. The anthropologists I kept encountering appeared to have a basic lack of confidence in their understanding of the subjects of their research. In methods classes we talked about the difficulties in ethnographic data collection due to differences in characteristics like gender, race, and age that arise between anthropologists and their interlocutors. I'm a white male.

One of my closest friends is an anthropologist named Satsuki Kawano—she's a Japanese female. Throughout our careers, Satsuki and I have studied very similar topics and have even done some fieldwork together in Japan. However, we do not collect the same data even when we ask the same questions. As an outsider, I can ask really stupid questions and will get a detailed response. The assumption is that I'm not Japanese, so of course I would ask simple questions about behaviors and objects that are perceived as being uniquely Japanese and, thus, outside of my cultural experience. If Satsuki asks the exact same questions, she is just as likely to get, "you're Japanese, you should know what it is" as she is to be presented with a detailed answer. But Satsuki is a native speaker of Japanese, I will never understand the answers to the questions I ask with the nuance with which she understands the answers to her questions, because my linguistic and cultural knowledge and skills will not permit that. Our genders as male and female also influence who will talk to us and what they will say, as well as what types of activities we can observe. I can visit a local woman's club; Satsuki can join that club. Perhaps the most powerful idea that came through in graduate school for me was the fact that regardless of how long one experiences the living situation of others, it is impossible to get into the heads of those people. Any understanding of how others see the world is inherently opaque. In anthropology, it seemed that I could still learn about why people do what others tell them to do, but I could do it in a way that recognized how things change and embraced the contingency of human experience and knowledge.

Anthropology is a very broad discipline—the word anthropology just means "study of humans" which leaves a lot of room for discovery. Traditionally, it has been broken into four fields: cultural anthropology, linguistic anthropology, physical anthropology, and archaeology. When you imagine

Jane Goodall and her decades-long study of social and family behaviors among wild chimpanzees, you are thinking about primatology, which is a sub-field in physical anthropology or the study of human and other primate biology and its connection to behavior. Linguistic anthropology focuses on the relationship between language and behavior and archaeology explores human social organization from the distant past using the material remains ancient people left behind. I'm a cultural (sometimes social is also used) anthropologist, meaning that I study ideas and behaviors that can be viewed as characterizing a particular group of people in the contemporary world. To put this another way, I study the lead sheet of a society and the ways in which people navigate and improvise off that lead sheet as they experience their lives on a daily basis. This is a messy business, because the boundaries of cultural lead sheets are exceptionally porous and often exist in a state of dynamic disharmony where tensions resolve only to generate new tensions, and the centuries-old process of globalization has led to constant interpenetration, hybridization, and elimination of many culturally imagined groups and ideas.

The method cultural anthropologists use to do research is known as ethnography, which also refers to the written products of our data collecting endeavors. I do ethnographic fieldwork, from which I write books called ethnographies that describe the lifeways and ideas of the people with whom I live and interact, which in my case is focused on a small town in northern Japan. Ethnographic methods involve living for a very long time in a cultural context usually distinct from one's own. For my dissertation, I spent a year and a half living in a fascinating village populated largely by descendants of samurai who a few hundred years ago protected their feudal domain from the one just to the north. As a native of the metropolitan Boston area, this was different from my experiences not only because I was in Japan, but also because I was living in an agricultural region as opposed to a metropolitan center—and the patterns of life are often quite distinct in agricultural regions as compared to cities, although in contemporary Japan, it is becoming increasingly difficult to view urban and rural lifeways as being significantly dissimilar (Traphagan, 2020). The reason given to graduate students for long-term fieldwork in another society is that living in an alien environment has a way of shaking up one's assumptions about what is normal and abnormal, true and untrue. There are significant intellectual advantages that arise from being a stranger in a strange land, and long-term fieldwork has a way of disrupting internalized beliefs and thoughts that display certainty. One's thinking becomes decreasingly structured in terms of blacks and whites, instead forming a kind of sloppy mosaic executed in shades of gray.

Anyone who has studied a second language will have encountered this feeling at least to some degree, and if it was a language quite different from their native one, it becomes obvious that people from different cultures don't think about the world in consistent ways. A good example of this can be found in the seemingly unambiguous practice of counting. One might imagine that people in all societies count things in largely the same way. I have one pen or two pens; one car or three cars; one dog or five dogs. If you look carefully at the last sentence, you'll notice that English speakers seem to feel a strong need to differentiate between one thing and more than one thing. That's why we add an "s" to the end of words when we are talking about multiple things. The use of singular and plural is so natural to us that we don't usually imagine there could be any other way to think about the things we count. I have no idea why we do this. In fact, the more I have thought about it, the more I've realized that it seems completely arbitrary. I could just as easily say one beagle and five beagle and you would understand what I mean.

Japanese people don't count like English speakers do. For one thing, they generally don't worry about singular and plural forms. One dog, two dog, three dog; there is nothing to indicate a difference between one as opposed to more than one. It's possible to form plurals in Japanese, but counting doesn't involve that. Instead, when people count, they usually indicate characteristics of the thing being counted such as size, use, or shape of the object. The table that follows shows an example of how this works.

Object	Japanese	English Meaning
Dog	一匹、二匹、三匹	One small animal, two small animals, three small animals
Cow	一頭、二頭、三頭	One large animal, two large animals, three large animals
Sheet of paper or a compact disk	一枚、二枚、三枚	One thing flat thing, two thing flat things, three thin flat things
Book	一冊、二冊、三冊	One volume, two volumes, three volumes

As you can see, for Japanese things in the world have various counters that describe the object. If you look at the kanji characters in the middle column, you can figure out which one represents the number of things being counted (this is only easy for the numbers 1 through 3, four looks like this 四); the second kanji character is the counter used for the object in the column on the left. Cylindrical objects have different counters from flat objects. Large machines have their own counters. The counter used for animals depends on the size of the animal. It's a very long list with over a hundred different counters, and the point to be taken from this is that Japanese don't think about counting the way English speakers do. They don't worry about one vs. many, but they do worry about the size, shape, or function of the object being counted. Large numbers are also organized differently from those in English. There is a word for 10,000 in Japanese. It's "man". 100,000 is jū-man or ten ten-thousands. One million is hyaku-man, or one-hundred ten-thousands, and ten million is issen-man or one-thousand ten-thousands. I'm able to count in Japanese, but conceptually the counting system doesn't enter my head well. I don't think in terms of the size and shape of the object being counted; I simply have memorized the counters for different objects. And I usually fumble when trying to indicate a very large number of something, like twenty-million dollars. I must stop and think about it to get the right word out, because the Japanese language doesn't organize the numbers in the way that English does and counting is something that we learn very early in life and come to experience as natural and normal at a deep level of experience.

What anthropology teaches is that the ability to empathize, or at least sympathize, with the perspectives of others lies in careful listening to the stories they convey, while trying to release one's own assumptions about natural or normal ways to organize the world. This can be quite difficult to do, even for people who are sympathetic to the experiences, and often suffering, of others. When the demonstrations in the US over the George Floyd murder of 2020 happened, members of my academic department were quick to post a statement online, which largely focused on stating that we recognize the racist history of the academy, which was sort of another way of saying we aren't racists. I showed it to my biracial kids, both of whom shook their heads and said, "they don't get it, it's not about telling, it's about listening." If we listen to the voices of others and try to understand this complex array of approaches and strategies that humans employ to categorize their world, the study of other cultures has a way of humbling the student—the normal and natural can be upended as he recognizes that the way those people over there organize their ideas and responses to the world has a logic that in its own way makes sense to them just as much as the logic of one's own way of doing things makes sense to the observer.

This isn't only true for those who live in foreign lands and exotic cultures—it's equally the case for people in our own society who view the meaning of life and the nature of truth in ways unlike our own. I don't have a particularly positive impression of evangelical Christianity; the unwavering conviction that ideology holds about the truth—and the only truth—related to our world and about ethics seems arrogant and destructive to the creation of a civil society. But I also recognize that there is a logic to the evangelical way of thinking that begins with assumptions about the world with which I don't agree—I don't believe in the existence of the Abrahamic deity; therefore, I don't have any use for the idea that moral truth emanates from the words attributed to that deity. But it is possible that I'm wrong and, more importantly, by trying to understand the logical framework, or the lead sheet, that stimulates and regulates evangelical belief I can come to understand the riffs and licks that fundamentalist Christians use in coping with the world and addressing their own form of human suffering. I don't need to like it to try to understand that logic. It's there, whether I like it or not; and trying to understand that logic and its emotional content opens the door to making the world at least somewhat safer for diverse views and attitudes, even if some of those attitudes are not particularly open to the very idea of diversity. To deeply experience the ways of thinking and acting among a different group of people and accept that there are alternate ways of constructing and interpreting any given cultural lead sheet, is to have one's convictions profoundly undermined. And that is a good thing.

3

MEETING DOGEN

One of the things that is realized when you see the nature of
the self is that what you do and what happens to you are the
same thing.

— *John Daido Loori (Kraft, 2018)*

uring my first semester at Pitt, I took a course on Buddhism in East Asia. One of the books assigned for the class was *Zen Master Dogen,* by Yuho Yokoi, which offered an introduction to one of the great thinkers in Japanese history. Dogen Zenji was a monk who lived between the years 1200 and 1253 and was ordained at the age of thirteen in the Tendai School of Buddhism on Mt. Hiei, just northeast of Kyoto. By the time he reached the ripe old age of fourteen, he was beginning to doubt one key aspect of Buddhist teaching. In Japanese Buddhism, as with other forms, there is a tradition of wrestling with a basic problem of understanding the meaning of Buddha-nature. The Buddhist monk Nichiren (1222-1282), a contemporary of Dogen, focused on the *Lotus Sutra* as the exclusive means to attaining enlightenment and saw Buddha-nature as "the inner potential for attaining Buddhahood" common to all living things. I don't know if they ever met, but I do know that they shared the generally accepted Buddhist sensibility that all things possess the Buddha-nature. Nichiren believed that the *Lotus Sutra* indicated all living beings possess the Buddha-nature and, therefore, all living beings have the capacity to attain Buddhahood or a state of awakening filled with compassion and deep understanding. For Nichiren, the Buddha-nature could be revealed in one's lifetime through the chanting of the Lotus Sutra. Other ideas about the Buddha-nature were floating around in intellectual circles during Dogen's formative years—in fact, Nichiren was not born until Dogen had already encountered and expressed his intellectual conundrum—but Nichiren's ideas reflect nicely the hang-up Dogen saw with common interpretations of Buddhism during his era that emphasized rigorously pursued behaviors like chanting or engaging in esoteric ritual practices as is common in Tendai Buddhism. Dogen's issue with the Buddhism he saw around him can be phrased as a simple logic problem: If everyone already has the Buddha-nature, why do people need to train rigorously to attain the Buddha-nature or to attain enlightenment?

In other words, why bother working diligently to attain enlightenment, when we already are enlightened? The problem was based on Dogen's reading of Buddhism and Buddha-nature in which the true nature of reality and Being-as-impermanence and the universe itself are understood as a vast emptiness that is the very expression of Buddha-nature. This meant that not only did humans have the Buddha-nature, but trees, dogs, grass, cockroaches—everything—has it. Or perhaps better, they *are* the Buddha-nature, which is impermanency itself. The grass, the clouds, the rivers of our world are the Buddha-nature, as is the impermanency of the human experience of things like mind and body, love and despair. In fact, for Dogen, in a somewhat mind-bending twist, enlightenment itself is impermanent because it is the Buddha-nature.

It may be simple, but Dogen's question is quite powerful; it challenges the foundations of Buddhist practice as well as basic human sensibilities about the world as consisting of differentiated parts in which individual selves are distinct islands of consciousness. According to most Buddhist thinkers of the time, to attain enlightenment one must do things like meditation or the practice known as *shikan* in Tendai Buddhism, or contemplating and chanting the *Lotus Sutra* in Nichiren Buddhism. But if you already have the Buddhanature, why bother? No good answers were forthcoming from his teacher at the monastery where Dogen lived on Mt. Hiei, so he left. After drifting from one temple to another, Dogen landed at Kennin-ji in Kyoto, where he asked Eisai Zenji his question. Eisai answered in an interesting way: "All the Buddhas in the three stages of time are unaware that they are endowed with the Buddha-nature, but cats and oxen are well aware of it indeed." Right. To put this another way, Buddhas— the enlightened—don't think in terms of binaries of having or not-having the Buddha-nature. In fact, that kind of thinking is what generates suffering and among humans, it's only the animal-like of the world who think in terms of these binaries. Note that to say someone is animal-like in Buddhism is not the insult it typically implies in Abrahamic societies. In Buddhism, humans are animals and all living things are valued. The main difference is that humans happen to be at a point on the wheel of *samsara*—the wheel of births and rebirths—that allows them to recognize the possibility of enlightenment and to search for the means to achieve it through jumping off of the wheel. The fact that we happen to have the potential for that awareness does not make humans better than other animals, just different.

Eisai's comment hit Dogen hard, and he decided to enter the Rinzai Zen sect that Eisai led; however, his mentor died not long thereafter, which threw something of a monkey wrench into Dogen's plans. Dogen persevered and went on to study Zen under one of Eisai's disciples, but after several years still found himself seeking a satisfactory answer to his question. At the age of twenty-three, he left for China along with his teacher Myozen to further their study of Zen. As Yokoi notes in his book on Dogen, when they arrived at the port of Mingchou, it took some time to find an appropriate temple for their studies so Dogen stayed aboard the ship for a few days. It was there he ran into a *tenzo* monk, a monk in charge of kitchen supervision at a nearby temple, who had stopped at the ship to buy mushrooms. Their conversation revolved around the monk's dedication to his work in the kitchen. Perhaps somewhat exasperated by the monk's single-minded focus on mushrooms, Dogen asked why he spent so much time doing kitchen work rather than sitting in *zazen* or studying the words of ancient masters. The old monk laughed at Dogen and admonished him indicating he lacked any understanding of the true training and meaning of Buddhism. Dogen asked for an explanation and in return received a cryptic comment along the lines of "if you knew what your question meant, you'd know the answer."

In other words, from the perspective of the old monk, Dogen was clueless.

One of the courses I teach is called Zen in the Western Imagination. I usually assign a book called *Zen in the Art of Archery*, first published in 1948 by German philosopher and Nazi, Eugen Herrigel (Herrigel, 1989). There is a good chance that if you are reading this book, you've encountered Herrigel's brief dive into Japanese archery, because it is among the most widely translated and read books ostensibly about Zen and it spawned an entire industry of "Zen in the art of…" publications, most of which are worthless in terms of presenting anything meaningful about Zen. In fact, Herrigel's book is largely worthless as a study of Zen, although I find it quite interesting as a study of how a Western philosopher interested in mysticism might interpret—or mis-interpret—behaviors and ideas expressed by someone in a culture he already thought was mystical as expressed through what he viewed to be the martial spirit of Japan.

Herrigel spent time near the city of Sendai in the 1920s, not far from my own research site, learning archery from an individual named Awa Kenzo, a successful archer who started a school and espoused some rather strange ideas about archery. Awa developed an idea, taken from one of his teachers, that "nothing is needed" when it comes to shooting an arrow. In its original form, this meant eventually one can simply focus on shooting, but at the beginning when one knows nothing it is important to learn the proper technique, particularly the proper stance. Apparently, Awa somehow concluded that "nothing is needed" meant the archer does not need to focus on technique at all—just shoot and things will mystically work out. Most of Awa's peers in the archery world thought he was at minimum odd and more likely an idiot and some even threw rocks at him when he passed. Recent research on Awa and Herrigel leave it ambiguous whether Awa actually associated his ideas as an archer with Zen, but for Herrigel, who already wanted to believe in Japanese and Zen mysticism, it was a match made in heaven.

Before his trip to Japan, Herrigel studied theology at the University of Heidelberg and was particularly interested in the mystical ideas of Meister Eckhart; it was this fascination with mysticism that seems to have drawn him to Zen, which he believed to be highly mystical even before he departed Germany. Herrigel had a variety of roadblocks that influenced his path to learning about Japanese religious and philosophical ideas. He didn't know the language very well, which meant he had to work through a translator (who, incidentally, in the 1960s confided that Awa's comments about archery were so weird that he was rather relaxed in his interpretations and sometimes just made things up he thought Herrigel would like). As the Japanese historian Yamada Shoji wrote in his excellent book about *Zen in the Art of Archery*, "Herrigel, influenced by D.T. Suzuki and driven by his own 'preoccupation with mysticism,' tried as hard as he could to detect Zen elements within Japanese culture" from which he mystified both Zen and Japanese archery, stimulating a profound misunderstanding of Japanese archery and of Zen that persists into the present in western societies (Yamada, 2011). My wife is an archer, and it irritates her considerably when she hears Americans interested in Japanese archery spouting convoluted, mystical ideas about what they are doing. Form is very important in archery, not because of some ritualized or mystical inner calm, but because good form leads to control which leads to good shooting. And, in any case, for most Japanese, archery is a sport that they play in high school and may continue later in life, much like some Americans continue to play baseball or softball as hobbies in adulthood. It doesn't have much of anything to do with Zen for people like my wife.

Yamada notes that Herrigel spent quite a bit of time trying to get Awa to explain his ideas about archery, to which Awa obliged with strange and difficult Japanese phrases. The most notable of these was Awa's comment "it shoots" as in the arrow shoots, somehow on its own. Yamada believes the original Japanese was most likely something along the lines of *sore deshita*, which he thinks Herrigel translated as "it shoots." I have no idea how one would say "it shoots" in Japanese, in part because there is no word for "it" in the language. The word for "shoot" when using an arrow in Japanese is *iru* (射る). Because Japanese don't usually use personal pronouns when they speak, to say "*iru*" is to say "shoot." That's it. It's just how the language works. The pronoun such as I, you, or it, is assumed in the context of conversation and if Awa said *sore irimashita*, it would mean "that shot" and would apply to something that shot the arrow, such as an automatic archery machine, if such a device were to exist. It's all very difficult to translate directly into English, or German, but there's nothing mystical about any of this. The Japanese language just works grammatically in a way very different from English and German, which are similar, and often can have a degree of ambiguity about who or what is doing an action. Herrigel seems to have infused a mystical ethos into what he was seeing and having interpreted for him as he studied with Awa but didn't really understand the nuances of Japanese grammar and, thus, probably didn't understand much of what he was being told—if Yamada is right, Herrigel employed a fair amount of poetic license in his interpretations.

Yamada argues that the confusion lies in Herrigel's intent upon finding mystical meaning in Awa's ideas and actions that would confirm his pre-existing ideas about Zen and Japan. Yamada argues, convincingly, that Herrigel had no idea how to deal with the phrase *sore deshita*, so he just created "it shoots" to represent something he completely misunderstood. If that was the phrase Awa used, then it just means "that's it" and there is nothing particularly mystical about it. If anything, it might have been used as praise when Herrigel managed to hit the target or display proper form. It was a pat on Herrigel's mystical German head.

Yamada offers two possible explanations for Herrigel's poor translation:
1. there was some sort of miscommunication between Awa and Herrigel related to "it shoots"; or
2. Herrigel just made the "it shoots" doctrine up when he wrote *Zen in the Art of Archery*.

And, as Yamada points out, Herrigel would have had some motivation in supporting the mystical interpretation of Japanese archery and tying it to Zen, because high ranking members of the Nazi Party, like Heinrich Himmler, were fascinated by Eastern mysticism. I'm not a historian, but it's clear that whatever Herrigel's intentions, his work on Zen helped him rise in Nazi Germany. He joined the Nazi Party in 1937, gave public talks about the martial spirit and mystical basis of Zen during the Nazi era, and was promoted to rector (president) of Erlangen University in 1945.

Regardless of how it helped his career, when it came to Zen Herrigel was clueless in a way that makes the young Dogen seem remarkably astute despite the admonition of the cook-monk purchasing mushrooms, and Herrigel's writing reflects very little of either the Japan or an understanding of Zen I have come to know over the years. This is not to say that Herrigel's ideas are uninteresting—I find them fascinating. But it's unfortunate that the book became a major contribution to Western ideas about Zen. Among the many equally clueless "Zen in the art of..." books that have been published since Herrigel's, the one that stands out as being remarkably clued-in probably has a title one would expect to be the opposite. That book is Robert Persig's *Zen and the Art of Motorcycle Maintenance* (Pirsig, 1974). With perhaps the exception of some of Alan Watts' writing, I can think of no other popular book by a western author that captures Japanese ideas about Zen, particularly as expressed by thinkers like Dogen, as well as Pirsig's, although there are some outstanding works by and about western Zen teachers that reflect Japanese Zen effectively, such as Richard Bryan McDaniel's *Cypress Trees in the Garden* (McDaniel, 2015).

"Care and Quality," wrote Pirsig, "are internal and external aspects of the same thing. A person who sees Quality and feels it as he works is a person who cares. A person who cares about what he sees and does is a person who's bound to have some characteristic of quality." When I first read this passage, I thought of Japan. Many Japanese practices, from making pottery to hitting a baseball to maintaining social relationships, are expressed and experienced with this type of non-dualistic identification in the ongoing practice of human experience as the interpenetration of care and quality. Dogen explored a very similar idea when he explained the meaning of identification as "nondifferentiation—to make no distinction between self and others...Identification is like the sea, which does not decline any water no matter its source, all waters gathering, therefore, to form the sea." This idea is closely tied to compassion, which is a practice that dissolves the barriers between self and other (Jenkins, 1999).

Both Pirsig's and Dogen's ideas, in my view, capture an important aspect of Zen and Japanese society—that self and other are mutually constructed and reflective. When it comes to daily life, this idea is expressed in terms of a sense of sincerity with which one gives or offers of oneself to the things one does and the others with whom one interacts. When it comes to Zen, this is found in the sense not that all things *have* the Buddha-nature, but that all things *are* the Buddha-nature, in all of its impermanence.

It's common among people in Western societies to associate Zen with meditation, which is often connected to the currently popular idea of mindfulness. This is not entirely wrong, but as it was presented by Dogen, Zen has little to do with meditation *per se*. I pulled this bit from a website focused on meditation in Buddhism: "One of the many benefits of Zen meditation is that it provides insight into how the mind works. As with other forms of Buddhist meditation, Zen practice can benefit people in myriad ways, including providing tools to help cope with depression and anxiety issues. The deepest purpose is spiritual, as the practice of Zen meditation uncovers the innate clarity and workability of the mind. In Zen, experiencing this original nature of mind is experiencing awakening."[5]

This is all interesting, but it doesn't have much to do with Zen as it is understood and practiced at least within the Soto School in Japan—it's one form of American Zen, which is a philosophy that has developed over the past century to become distinct from its Japanese and other East Asian origins. There are several important differences when it comes specifically to Dogen's Zen. For example, it is not intended to provide "benefits" nor is it aimed at giving people tools to cope with problems like anxiety or depression. This will sound weird, but Zen in the sense that Dogen understood it isn't aimed at anything. And, most importantly, it isn't spiritual. In fact, it was this approach to Buddhism that made Dogen's ideas a radical alternative to the Rinzai School and can be understood perhaps somewhat more clearly through his views on life and death. He wrote that "life does not obstruct death, and death does not obstruct life." As the contemporary Japanese thinker Masao Abe notes, this can be understood as the existential transcendence

---

5   https://mindworks.org/blog/what-is-zen-meditation-benefits-techniques/, accessed 16 April 2021.

of living and dying in which we realize that, in the present, both life and death are absolute in the moment (Abe, 2003). Living and dying co-construct—there can be no living without dying and no dying without living. We are always living and dying at any given moment of experience. The implication is clear; enlightenment, nirvana, is ever-present in the coming and going of birth and death. And if that's the case, then there is no aim at which to point in order to find enlightenment—it's immediately before us in every moment of our existence.

Before I explain this any further, I should make one point about Zen in Japan—for most Japanese Zen Buddhists, their practice has nothing to do with meditation, spirituality, or enlightenment. Zen for most Japanese who belong to one of its sects is about taking care of the dead, which is the way most of Buddhism works in Japan. When I did my fieldwork in the mid-1990s, I lived in a village populated largely by members of the Soto Zen sect—the sect Dogen created and the largest of the three Zen sects in Japan. The residents were Zen Buddhists not because of any commitment to the philosophy, but because they are descendants of the samurai class and that class was typically associated with Zen temples in terms of their religious affiliation. The people with whom I lived were Zen Buddhists because there is a Zen temple in the village, and that's where their family graves have been located since samurai times—there is no necessary reason for membership in this particular Buddhist sect based on religious or philosophical commitment. Nor do people in that village express their belonging to the temple in terms of spiritual or philosophical ideas—it is important to them primarily in relation to carrying out needs of the community associated with death.

A very good friend of mine is a Zen priest and we've spent many hours drinking beer, eating barbeque (which he loves), and talking about Buddhism. Like other Buddhist priests in Japan, most of my friend's time is spent taking care of the family business. That business is his temple, which is situated far up in the mountains a good half-hour drive from the nearest shopping area. His wife hates it. The work of the family business, which he inherited from his father and of which he is an employee, is to take care of funerary rituals for the members of the temple parish. Like most Buddhist priests I've met in Japan, my friend doesn't meditate. As far as I know, he also does not regularly sit in *zazen*, which is the word used in Japanese Buddhism to express the practice many outside of Japan conceive as meditation. We've talked a little about it and he told me that it makes his knees hurt—he has very long legs.

For most Japanese, the practice of Zen is not about meditation or about anything spiritual; it's about ritually caring for the dead and ensuring that the dead, whatever and wherever they are, stay alive in the minds and hearts of the living. Most of the people with whom I've spoken about the dead in Japan don't have very strong ideas as to whether or not there is an afterlife, but they do have a sense of identification between themselves and their ancestors. And sitting quietly before the Buddhist family altar in one's home can be a source of peace as one brings to mind the sources of one's own existence. One is what they were, and one is *because* they were. Therefore, it's important to keep something of the ancestors alive in the minds and hearts of the living. That's what ancestor memorialization is about for most Japanese. And for most Japanese Zen is about ancestor memorialization.

Of course, there are those who find themselves attracted to the more esoteric side of Buddhism and become engaged in chanting sutras or reading the philosophical treatises of thinkers like Dogen. My wife's grandfather did this—he wasn't a member of a Zen sect, but he chanted Buddhist sutras every day in his later life. Some people even meditate. But for Dogen, meditation was not part of Zen. That word, *zazen*, that is often represented in English as referring to meditation means to sit. It doesn't mean to meditate. It doesn't mean to learn about the workings of one's mind. It means to sit. Just sit. Nothing else. There's nothing mystical going on; it's just sitting. And there is no requirement that one sit. One can do standing Zen, squatting Zen, cutting tomatoes Zen. It really doesn't matter. It also doesn't matter that one sit for any particular length of time. As Watts put it, "A cat sits until it is done sitting, and then gets up, stretches, and walks away."

That comment by Watts captures nicely this way of thinking about Japanese Zen and brings me back to Dogen and his ideas about cooking for monks. Among the most important of Dogen's contributions is an essay called *Tenzo Kyokun, Instructions for the Head Cook*.[6] The treatise is exactly what you would expect. It explains how to prepare meals for the monks at a monastery. But right at the beginning, Dogen makes an interesting point: "Those without way-seeking mind will not have good results, in spite of their efforts..." What I think he means by this is that if you don't listen to what the world is telling you, you won't get Zen, and you won't be a very good cook, either. It's just like improvising in jazz; if you don't listen to the other musicians with whom you are creating a particular reality, it's impossible to make good music. By this, I am differentiating listening to music within the context of mutual improvisation from listening as an observer, although in reality the observer is also part of the performance. To be within the musical performance and to be listening to the other musicians is to be inside the musical conversation as opposed to eavesdropping on a conversation from the outside. You listen to what that world—the context of the performance—tells you as you listen to each other and improvise a novel, and yet ephemeral, reality in the moment.

Dogen goes on to describe how to prepare the food with care and quality:

> The cycle of one day and night begins following the noon meal. At this time the *tenzo* should go to the administrator and assistant administrator and procure the rice, vegetables, and other ingredients for the next day's morning and noon

---

6   https://wwzc.org/dharma-text/tenzo-kyokun-instructions-tenzo, accessed 31 March 2021.

meals. Having received these things, you must care for them as you would the pupils of your own eyes.... The *tenzo* handles all food with respect, as if it were for the emperor; both cooked and uncooked food should be cared for in this way.

Do not just leave washing the rice or preparing the vegetables to others but use your own hands, your own eyes, your own sincerity. Do not fragment your attention but see what each moment calls for; if you take care of just one thing then you will be careless of the other.

Be careful of sand when you wash the rice, be careful of the rice when you throw out the sand.

After cooking the vegetables for the morning meal and before preparing rice and soup for the noon meal bring together the rice pots and other utensils and make sure that everything is well-ordered and clean. Put whatever goes to a high place in a high place and whatever goes to a low place in a low place so that, high and low, everything settles in the place appropriate for it. Chopsticks for vegetables, ladles, and all other tools should be chosen with great care, cleaned thoroughly, and placed well.

Do not despair or complain about the quantity of the materials. Throughout the day and night, practice the coming and going of things as arising in the mind, the mind turning and displaying itself as things.

The *tenzo* should always be present at the sink when the rice is being soaked and the water measured. Watching with clear eyes, ensure that not a single grain is wasted. Washing it well, place it in the pots, make a fire, and boil it. An old teacher said, "Regard the cooking pot as your own head, the water your own life-blood."

If this doesn't sound particularly mystical, it's because it isn't. What Dogen is getting at is a rather simple idea that can be quite difficult to achieve—do one thing and only one thing at a time. He would not have been a fan of multi-tasking. This is why zazen isn't meditation in the sense of awakening the mind or gaining benefits to help with anxiety or depression. In fact, the point of this passage is simple: When you cut cucumbers, cut cucumbers. When you wash rice, wash rice. When you play jazz, play jazz. When you sit, sit. And with all of these things do them with care, which arises by not fragmenting your attention into things like exploring your mind or seeking benefits, but instead involves seeing and doing what each moment demands of you. I have no doubt that achieving this state would help with anxiety and depression, but that isn't the aim of Zen. And if I grasp what Dogen is getting at correctly, it's clear that if you engage in Zen practices with the goal of resolving feelings of anxiety or depression, you won't succeed. Goals generate differentiation and differentiation contributes to suffering.

Dogen's idea has affinities with the concept of mindfulness that has become popular in many Western societies. As I understand it, mindfulness involves being present and aware, as opposed to overly attentive to distractions. As one website on mindfulness puts it:[7]

> Whenever you bring awareness to what you're directly experiencing via your senses, or to your state of mind via your thoughts and emotions, you're being mindful. And there's growing research showing that when you train your brain to be mindful, you're actually remodeling the physical structure of your brain.
>
> The goal of mindfulness is to wake up to the inner workings of our mental, emotional, and physical processes.

---

7   https://www.mindful.org/meditation/mindfulness-getting-started/, accessed 5 April 2021.

There is much to be said about this approach to life, but one thing that cannot be said is that this reflects Japanese Zen in any significant way. The reason is because of the dualism inherent in the way this is presented— "whenever you bring awareness to what you're directly experiencing via your senses...you're being mindful...the goal of mindfulness is to wake up to the inner workings of our mental, emotional and physical processes." This way of thinking is quite far from Dogen's idea of nondifferentiation. In this view of mindfulness, there is an "I" that is doing something to its objectified self—that objectified self becomes an Other on which the I works. Dogen, by contrast, adopts a traditional Mahayana idea of nonduality/ absolute emptiness embodied in single-minded sitting, which is sitting without thinking—without doing something else. The achievement of authentic selfhood for Dogen is found in the radical dissolution of otherness experienced as the emptying of self-other duality. This authentic selfhood occurs in sitting. It occurs in cutting cucumbers and in cleaning rice. It occurs in playing jazz. The idea is not that there is an I doing something designed to wake up to some internal, or eternal, self—it is to simply be the moment and nothing else. When I play jazz, I *am* the performance of the music. There is a merging of quality and care through embracing emptiness, the radical dissolution of subject and object in the *doing* of something with complete presence. This isn't mindfulness; it's mindlessness or the dissolution of self. This sounds painfully like a binary, but I'm not sure how to express the idea in words without creating that sense of polar opposition. As I view it, the word mindfulness generates a sense of being *with* oneself, but in Zen, enlightenment is conceptualized in terms of the idea of no-self discussed by Japanese philosophers like Keiji Nishitani (Nishitani, 1990). This will sound annoyingly mystical, but the presence associated with western ideas about mindfulness is achieved in the elimination of mind as a perspective on reality.

Pirsig captures this idea nicely in fairly concrete terms when he talks about the difference between riding a motorcycle and riding *in* a car. I've never been on a motorcycle, but I have driven many snowmobiles and Pirsig's description sounds quite familiar to me:

> In a car you're always in a compartment, and because you're used to it you don't realize that through that car window everything you see is just more TV. You're a passive observer and it is all moving by you boringly in a frame. On a cycle the frame is gone. You're completely in contact with it all. You're in the scene, not just watching it anymore, and the sense of presence is overwhelming.

When you are just sitting, you are "in the scene" just like when you are only cutting cucumbers. In other words, when the subject/object, self/other dualism dissolves, we are no longer watching, but are present in that which we are doing and in the nondifferentiation of quality and care. Constructing the world in terms of dualities of right and wrong, good and evil, communist and capitalist, believer and atheist, and probably mindfulness/mindlessness, does quite the opposite of what Dogen describes. Rather than dissolving the binaries we tend to create in our struggles to cope with reality, these cultural tropes amplify our inattentiveness to identification and encourage an arrogant positionality grounded in a misguided notion that our world is one of consistencies rather than impermanence. It has the same disruptive quality as singing in D# major when everyone else is playing in E minor. It becomes impossible to collectively improvise off one's cultural lead sheet, which to do successfully demands a humble rejection of absolute convictions in favor of recognizing the contingent nature of what we know and experience.

4

HUMILITY

You've been making the wrong mistakes.
— *Thelonious Monk*

ver the years teaching in religious studies, I've had more than one student tell me that their parents had discouraged them from even taking a course in religious studies, because it would destroy their faith. Those parents are probably right if their kids take my classes; so it may make sense not to tell mom and dad too much about the strange and dangerous ideas one learns in college and that force us to think in new ways if we happen to be listening.

Of course, I think having one's faith challenged is a good idea. Certainty is unhealthy, because it closes the mind to change and, thus, to the world in which we live, rather than embracing the ever-evolving nature of our universe and ourselves. It's a mistake that derives from fear of the unknown and in many cases the arrogant unwillingness to be wrong. One of my favorite recent reads is *Points of Contact: Science, Religion, and the Search for Truth,* by Glenn Sauer (2020). I host a podcast for the New Books Network that focuses on books related to the study of science, technology, and society. I saw the title and thought it would be a good addition, so I invited Glenn to come on the podcast. When I received the book, I started to worry, because I found that not only is Glenn a biologist at Fairfield University, he's a committed Catholic and a spiritual director in the university's Murphy Center for Ignatian Spirituality. My fears about the interview stemmed from the fact that I usually don't get along well with committed Christians who are unwilling to entertain the possibility that their faith may be wrong or need occasional rethinking—creationists are a good example of this type of Christian. I worried that Sauer might fit into that camp and might want to talk about creationist topics like intelligent design as though they were not open to debate. Personally, I think humans arose through the Darwinian process of natural selection, but I'm willing to entertain a conversation about intelligent design, even if I don't see humans and other organisms on our planet as displaying much intelligence in terms of their design. If humans were designed, then the engineer who did it wasn't very good at their job. If you were going to set out to design a being that would do well, why not put eyes on the backs of our heads as well as the front? Leaving us with a gaping blind spot in back doesn't make much sense.

I could not have been more wrong about Glenn, a point that is captured well in this quotation from his book. Sauer writes that understandings "of God vary, therefore, from person to person and from age to age. They are always in flux because the true nature of God is impossible to know with the same kind of certainty with which we can describe physical reality," because "transcendent reality" as Sauer puts it, isn't verifiable using the methods we employ in the physical and social sciences to gain a feeling of certainty about our knowledge. This is an important point, because it recognizes that in order to be certain about the nature of a god, or even to be certain about its existence, one would have to be that god. Humans don't get a complete picture of anything they encounter in the world, so they can't obtain certainty about the nature of reality. As Sauer writes, this should essentially force upon us a humble willingness to accept that our knowledge—even of the Abrahamic God for Christians, Muslims, and Jews—is incomplete and open to revision over time.

In his discussion of the atheism of thinkers like Richard Dawkins, Sauer works through another important observation. He writes that scholars like Dawkins have "conflated the methodological naturalism of science with their own philosophical commitment to atheism" which leads to a form of scientific materialism in which any conversation about a nonmaterial reality is automatically rejected. This happens because atheist writers like Dawkins and Sam Harris refuse to acknowledge the fact that their own materialistic atheism is a philosophical commitment, rather than an empirical fact about the world.

I like the way Sauer thinks—and I'm a materialist agnostic with quite a bit of sympathy for atheism. I've long felt that thinkers like Dawkins and Harris have an important perspective (as does Sauer) that is needed to counter the certainty-driven, faith-based approach to reality and life pursued and pushed by groups like evangelical Christians or fundamentalist Islam. However, where I differ with the likes of Dawkins and Harris is on the certainty with which they proffer their perspectives on the non-existence of a god. As Sauer convincingly argues, the hard atheism of Dawkins is an expression of hubris just like the ideologies of conservative Christian groups or Islamic fundamentalists. Both perspectives lack a basic humility that fails to acknowledge the contingency of our knowledge about the world. Sauer, of course, sees the "certainty" of scientific investigation as inherently contingent and argues that one way to resolve, or at least begin to address, the gulf between religion and science in societies like the US is for both sides to approach dialogue with humility that recognizes the varied ways in which humans see and experience the world, as well as accepting the idea that truth is always changing in relation to the context of our knowledge and understanding of that which is.

The things we think are true today may be true in different ways at some other time or even come to be deemed wrong as our understanding reflects the changing world around us and the inherent incompleteness in our knowledge of reality. We no longer think the Earth is the center of the universe, but the Ptolemaic geocentric view of the universe wasn't just a crazy idea—it was based on observation and mathematical calculations that were reasonably good at predicting the movements of planets, although it was also a product of adding *ad hoc* mathematics to support a pre-existing theory (Vertesi, 2020). In fact, if you think about it, from a strictly observational perspective, the geocentric model makes better sense than the heliocentric model. Spend a day observing the location of the sun (without staring at it, of course) and it will appear that it moves across the sky from sunrise to sunset. Without the knowledge we have gained through modern science, the idea that the earth is moving around the sun would seem counter intuitive.

Ptolemy's geocentric understanding of the cosmos was true to the extent that human observations of the universe permitted at the time he developed his scientific ideas and it eventually became conflated with an absolutist ideology political leaders in the Catholic Church deemed necessary for preserving their positions of power. When thinkers like Copernicus and Galileo came along and challenged the geocentric model with both better math and new observations made possible by the invention of the telescope, more accurate representations of our universe in which the earth orbits around the Sun emerged. This change in perspective didn't happen overnight. Copernicus still accepted elements of Ptolemy's astronomy, but as more data were obtained human representations of our universe shifted from a geocentric to a heliocentric model. Of course, the old truth did not go down without a fight, but that was because it came into direct conflict with other truths related to aspects of human experience such as who should hold political power, how wealth should be distributed, and philosophical and religious assumptions about the source of moral and empirical authority. The heliocentric model of the solar system challenged much more than adherence to the geocentric model of the cosmos; it subverted attitudes about who should be in charge of deciding what is and isn't true by undermining certainty about the physical world. Should it be religious leaders like the Pope? Or should it be scientists like Galileo? This argument continues right into the present and is seen in the Trump administration's response to climate change and the COVID-19 pandemic in which the authority of scientific experts was continually called into question by those in political power. The Trump years can be characterized as a constant bimodal fight over who has authority to decide what is and isn't true.

The behaviors of the Trump administration, of course, were a nihilistic and cynical attempt to claim that truth is simply whatever those in power say it is. This is quite different from the idea that our understanding of truth is constantly changing in relation to our knowledge of the world. To say that our knowledge is limited and incomplete is to be reflexive about the seeming inability of humans to fully know anything. It is different from the arrogant claim to certainty about either the world or who should have power in the world and instead is a humble claim that we just can't know everything, regardless of how hard we try. Therefore, we will always be faced with uncertainty about what is true.

The shift from a geocentric to a heliocentric model of the cosmos can be understood as one of the context in which a "truth" is understood changed over time and with that change what was understood as true also changed, which implies that our knowledge about any truth should always be open to question and potentially to revision. You may be thinking, yeah, but our take on the solar system is more accurate than Ptolemy's was. Indeed. But to assume that we have a perfect understanding on how our solar system works is no different from people thinking Ptolemy did hundreds of years ago. At his time, the geocentric version was the best explanation of the movement of planets available and made sense; our current explanation is the best available now and makes sense—but it will continue to be refined. One difference is that modern science tends to generate refinements at a much swifter pace than the 1,500 years it took to get from Ptolemy to Copernicus. But refinement continues as we learn about our universe and our ideas related to how we should think about its features and nature continue to change—when I grew up, Pluto was a planet. Today it's a dwarf planet, although that classification continues to be debated among astronomers. Our understanding of the solar system is much better in the sense that we can predict things like the motions of planets today than it was in Ptolemy's time, but it isn't complete, and it never will be. We may reach a point that we decide we have a relatively complete understanding, but there will still be surprises and there also will still be all the other star systems out there about which we will know virtually nothing. To have a complete understanding of our solar system, we'd have to be the solar system.

This is a difficult pill to swallow if you believe that THE truth is knowable, and it's even more difficult if you think you already know that truth and there is no possibility you might be wrong. I have little need in my life for the god hypothesis—I find neither comfort nor peace-of-mind in the idea that some all-powerful being is watching what I do, has the ability to do anything it wants, and yet refuses to correct my endless string of stupidities and errors. It makes no sense to me. But I accept the possibility that such a being could exist, even if I think it highly unlikely, and as a result maintain a position of agnosticism in relation to the existence of any god. It's possible that the Japanese sun goddess Amaterasu is or was real—some have argued that she may, in fact, be in some way based on a real figure from human history. I doubt she was ever a deity beyond those characteristics other humans ascribed to her (if she was a real person), but I can't be 100% certain about her non-existence as a true deity any more than I can about the non-existence of the Abrahamic god. There is room for error and although I feel reasonably confident that neither of these deities exist or existed, I am not certain.

Richard Dawkins doesn't like this perspective and, in his book *The God Delusion*, he sums up the anti-agnostic position well when he discusses the ideas of English biologist Thomas Huxley, who was known for his support of Darwin's ideas, his discomfort with organized religion, and his agnosticism. In his critique of Huxley, Dawkins states that "existence of God is a scientific hypothesis like any other." It can be answered in a binary way—either the hypothesis is proved or disproved. God exists or God doesn't exist. Dawkins is right, of course, in his argument that there is a reasonable empirical question about the existence of the Abrahamic god that is worth considering, just as there is about any form of non-material being humans have believed to exist throughout their history. But the problem with Dawkins' position is that he fails to recognize the existence of anything—whether materially observable or not immediately accessible to direct human observation—is also an epistemological question. It is related to what we know and don't know, as well as what we *can* and *cannot* know and the methods through which knowledge is obtained. Scientific reason and faith are different epistemological positions that do not draw on the same methods for attaining knowledge. Dawkins argues forcefully that the scientific method is the *only* way to attain knowledge. Although I happen to privilege scientific reason over faith as a source of knowledge, it would be inaccurate to say I am certain I'm not wrong in doing this. Certainty that the scientific method is the only reliable and justifiable way to attain true understandings of the world and knowledge is no more possible than certainty that my dog is sleeping in the next room. I'm pretty sure she is—that is her usual state of existence—but she might have gotten up to get some food, which is another common activity. I'm not in that room. And if I were to consider what my dog is thinking about, I can only guess. If she heads to the kitchen, I suspect she is thinking about food, but the only way I could know for sure is if I were Chloe, the Shetland Sheepdog who lives in my house.

And because knowledge is contingent and changing along with the constant changes of the universe in which we live, it's pretty difficult to state in an intellectually reasonable way that

I'm certain no god exists, even if the Abrahamic god seems far-fetched from my particular perspective on the world. Frankly, I think the Abrahamic god of the Old Testament is something of an absurd figure. I tend to agree with Dawkin's negative assessment that as presented in the Old Testament he's not a particularly pleasant being and often behaves largely like a human toddler. When I think of the whole Noah's Ark episode, the image that comes to mind is of a four-year-old who builds a Lego city and then smashes it because he doesn't appreciate what he built. I think the existence of this kind of god to be unlikely, but I don't think it's impossible. The world is a weird place. If we live in a computer simulation as some scientists and philosophers have recently imagined,[8] maybe the Abrahamic religions got it right after all and we are just living our lives within the confines of a computer game being played by some super-powerful being like Star Trek's Q, who has the maturity level of a five-year-old.

Japanese Buddhism doesn't have deities like the Abrahamic god, and most Japanese represent themselves as non-religious, so this issue of a dualism between religion and science that Dawkins focuses on and that Sauer does a wonderful job navigating doesn't usually arise. Buddhism in Japan does have spirit beings, found in the form of ancestors and some other deity-like imagined entities. But generally speaking, there is no sense of an omniscient/omnipotent Creator Other god in Japanese Buddhism, although in some sects such as Jodo Shinshū, there are similarities in the sense that people take refuge in the Otherness of Amida Buddha as the embodiment of the Law of Buddhahood manifested in the name Amida, which is repeated in prayer with the idea that sincere recitation of the name will allow for entrance into the Buddhist Pure Land.

---

8   Anil Ananthaswamy. Do We Live in A Simulation? Chances Are about 50-50. *Scientific American*, 3 October 2020. https://www. scientificamerican.com/article/do-we-live-in-a-simulation-chances-are-about-50-50/, accessed 4 April 2021.

However, there are significant differences between Christianity and Shin Buddhism, particularly in the sense that the central problem for humans in Shin Buddhism, as is the case throughout the Mahayana tradition, is their ignorance of the true nature of the world, which consists in identity with the Absolute or the unity in everything represented in Amida as the elimination of our delusional subject/object polarity (Fox, 1968). In other words, Amida is a manifestation of the oneness of everything, as are all living beings, so identification with the "other" that is Amida becomes identification with the oneness that is everything.

For me, the fact that different religions like Buddhism and Christianity have arrived at rather distinct ideas about the nature and existence of non-material beings and their relationships to humans, suggests that humans really don't have much of a clue on this and it would be best to withhold judgment on the reality of such beings. Even if Dawkins is right that it's a question of which hypothesis we decide to support, the data don't seem to be sufficiently in evidence right now to draw a firm conclusion—a good scientist might have a hunch, but it's a mistake to draw conclusions about the verity of a hypothesis until you think you have sufficient data. And even when that moment occurs, it is essential in science to be open to the idea that the things one knows today are going to change; therefore, one's conclusions are probably going to have to change at some point, as well.

In Dogen's Zen, the experience of life isn't about getting at an objective, or objectified, truth or certainty about the world. It's about intimacy, not with a personal god, but intimacy experienced through identification with the world. In his *Shobogenzo* or *Treatise of the True Dharma Eye*, he writes: "Because 'the intimate is what is near you,' everything exists through intimacy; each half exists through intimacy. Personally investigate such fact with clarity and diligence in your practice." One way to understand this perspective is, perhaps, to think in terms of its opposite, which I think is expressed well by the Christian theologian Paul Tillich. "Being alive," writes Tillich, "means being in a body—a body separated from all other bodies. And being separated means being alone." I think that Dogen and Tillich might agree on the general assessment of our perceptions as being a feeling of separation from all that is around us and that this sensibility contributes to our experience of suffering. They would disagree, however, on the basis of that sensibility. For Tillich the separation is an ontological fact—an expression of what it is to be human—tied to what he refers to as the "bondage of time" and a sense of being trapped in guilt over those things we have done in our past and the intuition that there is an absolute truth from which our actions cannot be divorced. Individual humans are solitary and alone, trapped in the flow of time, but able to transcend our loneliness through entrance into the "eternity *above* time" found in the communion of prayer and worship (Tillich, 1963) I think. Tillich is a bit confusing. But as I read his ideas, he sees a binary between time and the eternal and humans live their lives within time as isolated beings. This binary is real, rather than an illusion as typically represented in Buddhism. For Dogen, the feeling of differentiational identity is an illusion generated by human clinging to the desire to achieve certainty about a world that is inherently uncertain. It's based on human misunderstanding of the way the world really is.

Dogen's emphasis on practice is important here. The intimacy he describes is found not by philosophizing about the nature of the world or humanity's place in the universe, nor in prayer to a deified Other, it's found through doing—practicing—our lives. Dogen conceptualizes practice in terms of gratitude for the kindness others exhibit toward us and the wisdom that has been conferred by the various Buddhas who have transmitted their understanding of the dharma—the nature of reality taught by the Buddha—from one generation to the next. He comments that the true way to express gratitude is through the doing of Buddhist practice selflessly and with esteem for each day we are in this world. To be selfless is to have humility, and to be humble is to be uncertain. It is to take a position that my understanding of anything observed is inherently incomplete; therefore, I cannot stake a claim to any capital T Truth about my observations of the world—whether scientific, religious, or philosophical. The only thing about which I may be able to have complete understanding is myself, because I know what it is to be me, and one of the things I know about being me is that I lack complete knowledge of anything other than me. I will admit that I'm not even sure I can have a full understanding of myself, since I keep changing.

When I teach about contemporary Buddhism in Japan, I make a distinction between philosophical and practiced Buddhism. As I mentioned earlier, for the average Japanese person, Buddhism is about memorializing the dead. My friend the Zen monk, his name is Taikan which is a Buddhist name that means "great relaxation," is always busy, ironically, because, due to the agedness of the Japanese population, there are a lot of people dying. This means he spends most of his time carrying out the mortuary rituals that characterize much of Japanese Buddhism. This does not mean, however, that the ideas associated with Zen and other sects of Buddhism in Japan, and particularly the notion of gratitude, do not influence the daily lives of people. Taikan has expressed to me that although he doesn't believe that ancestral spirits exist in any way beyond our own memories of the deceased—he sees death as an off switch—he does find the philosophy of Buddhism an appealing way to lead one's life. The emphasis on gratitude and humbleness is something he sees as good and certainly characterizes his personality and a life committed to awareness and concern for the needs of others. That's actually why he is a priest—it's not because of a belief in the spirit-beings of Buddhism, but because he inherited the work from his father. Taikan wanted to become a sociologist and studied for that in college. And despite not "believing in" the ancestral spirits—it is not necessary to believe in any sort of spirit being to practice religion in Japan (Traphagan, 2004)—he sees his role as a ritual leader helping others cope with the death of loved ones as important work. He cares greatly about the needs of his parishioners and has committed himself to doing his work as Buddhist priest with quality.

One of the features of Japanese life that has most impressed me is the other-oriented way in which many people, like Taikan, interact. Sometimes when I am in the town where I do research, I will drop by the office of the mayor and see if I can make an appointment to ask him questions about the current political situation of the town. He is always very obliging and if he isn't too busy, will usually just invite me into his office. We sit in the large chairs used for entertaining guests and one of the mayor's assistants will bring refreshments—green tea for the mayor and coffee for me. Twenty years ago, the coffee would always come with cream and sugar already blended in. Unfortunately, I hate sugar in my coffee, but I would drink it out of a desire to be polite. The decision of the mayor's assistant to prepare my coffee with sugar and cream added is a product of a tendency in Japanese society to want to anticipate the needs and wishes of others. At the time, it was thought Americans generally liked sugar in their coffee, so that's how coffee should be prepared for an American. Over the years, I've noticed that the awareness has changed, perhaps as more Americans have visited, and today both cream and sugar come on the side of my cup of black coffee. This example sums up much about Japanese life—people are carefully attuned to the needs of others. It is an example of what Pirsig means when he talks about Quality expressed in the mundane acts of daily life.

Japanese society produces people who are generally sensitive to their relationships with and the needs of others. The Japanese language tends to reinforce this by de-emphasizing the creation of binaries like self and other through the use of elements such as personal pronouns. For the most part, Japanese do not use personal pronouns in normal speech. If I am about to go to the store, I would say, "*mise ni iku*" which simply means "store to go". If I want to order you to go to the store, I say, "*mise ni ike*" which is a command, or I can ask by saying "*mise ni itte kudasai*"—store to go please. And if I want to suggest we go together, I would say, "*mise ni iko ka*" which means "store to go?" and can be translated as "shall we go to the store?" The word "ka" has no equivalent in English; it identifies a question and despite being a world, functions in the way that the question mark does as punctuation in English. I don't want to dive into the complexities of Japanese grammar. Rather, I use this to illustrate that in neither of these examples is there a personal pronoun used. The context of the conversation and the nature of the grammatical structure—the shift of *u* to *e* or *o* or the addition of *kudasai* is the key—indicate who is doing what; in the first case it is "I" and in the second "you" and in the third "we." Another example of this can be found in the way Japanese use the extension *-san*, which is gender-neutral and, thus, means Mr./Mrs./Ms./Mx. in English. If I call a company and ask for Takahashi-san, the person answering may respond, "hold on, I will get Takahashi." He may then turn around and call out, "Takahashi-san, phone!" What's happening here is that when talking to a member of an out-group (me) he doesn't use *-san*, which indicates that Takahashi is part of his in-group in relation to me as an outsider. But when he turns around—perhaps Takahashi is a superior—he attaches *-san* to note that they are not in the same in-group within the company. It's quite complex.

Japanese live in a fluid world in which identities shift in relation to the context of the social interactions through which they are moving at a given point in time. More and less polite forms of the language are used as people work through their social encounters and they will mix up these forms in the process of generating rapport with people they meet. One might be formal at first and then begin to throw in less formal structures or words as a way of saying, "I'd like to relax our relationship a bit."

There is also a powerful emphasis on the idea of gratitude, which in Buddhism is displayed via showing thanks to one's parents and one's ancestors—the people on whom your very existence is dependent. To show gratitude with sincerity, by doing things like ancestor rituals or caring for parents in old age, is to be engaged in the intimacy of life with others. Of course, Japanese people have a sense of individual self and people can be selfish in their behaviors—which is seen as morally wrong unless there's a good reason for it. But the overall ethos of Japanese culture is one in which people are and should be aware of the needs of others and willing to put those needs ahead of their own, particularly in situations where they have a connection to the others involved. The world is a place of social encounter and to be a person is to be constantly engaged in moving through a world characterized by varying degrees of intimacy in our relationship with others that need to be carefully navigated.

I think that if there is an influence on Japanese society from Buddhism—and I most certainly do think that—this would be the most notable one and it can be understood as the playing out in daily life of the idea of intimacy as a practice of gratitude and kindness towards others, both human and non-human. And like all philosophical influences on culture, these ideas shape individual behavior in various ways as people encounter and interpret the riffs and licks of Japanese culture, as well as those of other individuals living in the social and geographical space known as Japan and improvise novel ways of employing their own interpretations of ideas like gratitude as they co-construct social realities.

This sense of intimacy also leads to a downplaying of binaries. If you have an automobile accident in Japan, it's common for people to immediately apologize and claim it was their own fault. It isn't necessarily the case that they actually think they were at fault, but there is an assumption that most of the time when something goes wrong, the cause is not binary, but at some level the responsibility of both parties.

Because Japan is not a very litigious society, it's fine to claim some responsibility for any accident in which one is involved. It's unlikely that it will be perceived by either side as being entirely the fault of one of the parties, although in some cases, such as hitting a parked car, it will be. And it is also unlikely that there will be a lawsuit.

If you think about it, this makes a great deal of sense. Several years ago, I drove to campus and parked the pickup truck I owned at the time in a space near the building where I was to spend the day in the promotion and tenure committee for the College of Liberal Arts. This committee is tiring, as we usually are required to read the files of around 40 candidates for promotion prior to the meeting and then discuss the merits of each case in a marathon meeting that takes two days to complete. At the end of the day, I wandered, somewhat dazed with exhaustion, to my truck and backed out, hitting the Jaguar that was parked slightly below me, because the parking lot has a slope. I never even saw the car. As I was writing a note to place on her car, the owner came out and walked up to it, pulling off the ticket that was on her windshield. In an angry tone she said, "Did you put this on my car?" I have no idea why she would think I am a parking officer. I replied, "no, but I just backed into your headlight." She was having a very bad day. The ticket was there because she had parked illegally in a spot that isn't even a parking place. I assume that she did this because there were no available spaces and she didn't want to look elsewhere for a place to put her nice car. So, was I 100% at fault for backing into her parked Jaguar? In a way yes, but in a way no. I should have seen her car, but I also had no reason to expect a car would be parked outside of the normal parking spaces. If she had simply found an actual space in which to put her car, it never would have happened. In one sense, it was partially her fault because she chose to park her car in a place where no-one would expect it to be. She clearly saw the accident as entirely my fault—I think she even believed the ticket was somehow my fault—but in Japan most people would likely work through the situation in the way I did in this paragraph and assign some balance of fault among the two parties because the woman with the Jaguar had not taken the time to think about what others might do given the location of her car. She was only focused on her own needs. In any case, my insurance paid to fix her headlight and my rear bumper after I dropped $500 on the deductible. Oh well…I should have looked more carefully.

To determine who is at fault is less important for most Japanese than to sincerely take responsibility for whatever one might have done to contribute to a difficult situation. An accident is usually a moment co-constructed by both parties, therefore, both parties are likely to hold some level of responsibility for whatever happened. The context of an accident like the one I just described isn't thought of as involving a binary between who was right and who was wrong. I want to be careful to avoid over-stating this, however. In situations like the Fukushima nuclear power disaster, the Fukushima Nuclear Accident Independent Investigation Commission (NAIIC) placed blame squarely on energy utilities, regulators and the government, stating they "effectively betrayed the nation's right to be safe from nuclear accidents." Interestingly enough, even in this case the report created a level of ambiguity about the fault of the disaster when in his introductory note to the report, NAIIC Commission Chairman Kiyoshi Kurokawa stated regulatory failings leading up to the disaster were a direct product of "cultural characteristics" specific to Japan, including ingrained conventions of Japanese culture like "reflexive obedience" and "reluctance to question authority".[9]

Even in a situation in which those responsible for a problem are identifiable, some level of ambiguity can still be found. This, of course, is a result of the processes of socialization that for Japanese produce a self not constructed in terms of polar oppositions that juxtapose their own interests, attitudes, and expectations with those of other people. Japanese don't see

---

9   https://www.scientificamerican.com/article/fukushima-blame-utilities-goverment-leaders-regulators/, accessed 25 April 2021.

themselves as isolated entities but as beings embedded in layered social circles in which they are interconnected with others in varying degrees ranging from strangers to the inner circle of friends and family. Responses to encounters with others, including those that may involve conflict, do not occur outside of the context of constant co-construction of the social order. There is a kind of built-in uncertainty about that order because one never knows the relative status of others until it has been formally determined—this generates a kind of innate humility in one's encounter with others.

In her analysis of the 1980s comedy film *Tampopo* that contrasts Japanese and Western sensibilities as it follows a woman's quest to make perfect ramen noodles, anthropologist Emiko Ohnuki-Tierney argues that the nature of selfhood in Japan is built on a value system that refutes selfishness. She uses one scene in the movie, in which two lovers repeatedly transfer a raw egg between their mouths, to argue that the unselfish self is symbolized in the transfer of the egg. As the scene unfolds, that interdependent and unselfish self is extinguished when one of the lovers does something selfish—he breaks the yoke and swallows the egg. This is probably over-thinking the scene, but Ohnuki-Tierney is right in her argument that Japanese people are normally uncomfortable with highly self-centered behavior and typically view selfishness as morally unacceptable.

Japanese children are socialized to downplay self-centered actions, at least when they are interacting in peer groups at school or on the playground. A strong sense of conviction about getting one's way is termed *wagamama* (わがまま) and suggests unwarranted selfishness or arrogance on the part of the offending individual. Early in life, children are encouraged to show restraint in pursuing personal desires when those desires may affect others and to try to orient their own desires in ways that align or blend with the interests and wants of people in the social groups to which they belong. This should not be taken as meaning that Japanese somehow lack a sense of individualized self or that they do not engage in selfish behavior.

Japanese people can be highly individualistic, particularly when it involves maintaining independence and avoiding burdening others, an act that is also seen as morally problematic in large part because it, too, is perceived as being selfish even when that burden may come in the form of receiving care at the end of life. At times for Japanese, to be highly independent is the best way not to be selfish. But the Japanese take on individuality doesn't necessarily imply a sense of isolation. Instead, sociality is an inevitable component of individuality, just as individuality is an inevitable component of sociality. The two interpenetrate in a way that social solidarity and individualism end up co-constructing each other.

This observation points out one of the widespread stereotypes of Japanese society that is inaccurate. In a great deal of academic and other writing on Japan, the country is described as a collectivist society that contrasts with the individualism of societies like the US. In neither case is this an accurate description, but in relation to Japan it shows a failure to see the ways in which social solidarity and individualism are complementary aspects of Japanese identity. They are not viewed as being in binary opposition to each other. And for Japanese, the issue isn't whether or not one is individualistic or collectivistic; it is understanding the contexts in which self-oriented behaviors are and are not reasonable and acceptable and always keeping in mind that the things one does affect others. Again, there is no binary between individualist and collectivist mindsets in Japan—the two are interpenetrating aspects of the experience of living with other people. The issue for Japanese is not whether one favors an individualistic or collectivistic mode of living in society, but how one navigates the streams of individualism and collectivism that characterize social life.

Japanese people can be selfish, just like people everywhere, but this is not seen as necessarily a product of individualistic ideology. Self-centered behavior is considered inappropriate when it occurs in interactions with others, particularly when those others are remote from the innermost circles of relationships such as family or friends. When encountering people with whom they are less familiar, Japanese tend to withhold personal opinions or at least express them gently in an effort to remain situated within the ebbs and flows of co-construction of the social world. Each person exists as a mediation point between inner and outer worlds of experience, rather than as an isolated self set in binary relationships with equally isolated others. In this sense, Japanese inhabit a world of interactional, presentational selves that display both sympathy and empathy for other selves defined and sustained through the ongoing process of social intertwining.

Anthropologist Takie Lebra described Japanese experience as involving multiple self-concepts people use to express who they are in relation to various social contexts and to negotiate their relationships with others. I think this idea has close connections to Buddhist philosophy, although one should be careful in drawing too much in the way of conclusions when it comes to finding underlying influences in human cultures. Japan certain is heavily influenced by Buddhism, but there are other philosophical perspectives that have shaped Japanese culture some of which have been drawn from the mainland of Asia, some of which are indigenous, and some of which are products of contact with western societies like the US. It is far too easy to over-simplify or to use a word common in anthropology circles—to essentialize—any culture on the basis of a few common themes. I do think, however, that the idea of self for most Japanese is constructed in some sense in terms of the concept of no-self or being devoid of an enduring, concrete self, present at birth along the lines of Freud's Id. As a woman who lives in northern Japan, and with whom I've spoken for research purposes many times, explained, Japanese view the infant as something of a *tabula rasa* and the person you are *becomes* through social interaction. A person or self is continually co-constructed with others and who you are today will be different as you encounter others on another day. It's an ongoing process and people experience emotional and psychological pain when they are removed from that social process, as I described in my book *Taming Oblivion*. Selfish behavior is one of the things that can, depending on the situation, pull someone out of that process, leading to the experience of suffering, which from a philosophical Buddhist perspective is only alleviated through recognizing the illusion of the existence of an isolated, permanent, eternal self or soul. In other words, self is contingent.

I'm not convinced that most Japanese follow the doctrine of no-self in daily life in any conscious way, but I do believe that the doctrine influences Japanese tendencies to avoid thinking about themselves as isolated, permanent beings that should be or are instinctively concerned primarily with their own interests. At some level in Japanese society, the inner being of humans does not really involve a stable "I" or fixed core for self-identity and subjectivity that constantly exhibits specific desires and needs that are routinely in conflict with those of others and are stimulated to action through the setting of goals designed to attain ego-driven wants. Although personal desires certainly exist, and Japanese can and do pursue them, those tendencies are balanced by an unbounded sense of self as embedded in the Buddhist notion of disengagement from the dichotomies of the world and the identification of one's own identity with social and physical environments as non-distinct. This way of viewing the relationship between self and other can override an emphasis on inner-focused subjective desires and feelings of having a unique personal identity with outer-directed empathy toward the needs and feelings of others. But, again, when and how this happens depends on situation—context is everything in Japan.

The worldview related to thinking about identity I've just described has consequences for daily life. Japanese tend to disavow any firm sense that humans can act in truly autonomous or independent ways. Because to be human is to be inevitably embedded in an intimate interplay of sociality it's necessary for decision-making to be sensitive to the needs of others, as well as to the context in which personal interactions, including traffic accidents, happen. Ideas about what is right or wrong are not viewed as binaries built on an absolute Truth (that often comes into conflict with some other absolute Truth) but are tied to the situation in which a particular interaction happens that may cause conflict by transgressing on the interests of others and, thus, disrupting the harmonic structures of localized cultural lead sheets. To be selfish is generally seen as wrong. This is not based on the belief in an objective understanding of right and wrong, but because selfish behavior removes the individual from the interdependencies of social life and privileges personal desire over the needs of others. It represents a clinging to self and one's own desires that ignores the fact that those things only exist in relation to everything else in one's surrounding environment.

Another feature of Japanese values that is important and that reflects the Buddhist ideal of nonduality is evident in the fact that moral value—the feature of something being morally right or wrong—is tied to the context of action rather than to an action itself. This means that to judge the moral value of an act, one must understand the circumstances that stimulated a series of actions that may be of questionable moral value. I'm fairly convinced that if I were to ask someone in Japan to respond to the moral dilemma in which one is asked about the ethics of going back in time to kill Hitler as a child, thus saving millions of lives, I might obtain unequivocal affirmative answers to the question without a great deal of internal struggle over the moral content of the specific action of killing another person in the form of Adolf Hitler. The context in which so many died as a result of Hitler's actions and ideology would easily outweigh any concerns about taking one life. This is not to say that people wouldn't think about the dilemma and consider alternatives, but in the end the context would dictate the right course of action. As Takie Lebra explains her book

Japanese Patterns of Behavior: "The clear-cut dualism of good and bad, right and wrong that is characteristic of unilateral determinism is not congenial to the Japanese sense of morality. For the Japanese, goodness or badness is a relative matter, relative to social situation and impact..." The impact of removing the consequences of Hitler seem unambiguously positive in terms of saving lives, therefore it would be right—or at least not wrong—to take him out.

Japanese don't usually see right and wrong in terms of binary opposition but view the idea of the good at least in part as arising out of a transcendence of the duality between objectivity and subjectivity through the awareness of the beauty of an event or act. As such, moral truth coincides with virtue conceptualized as an aesthetic and emotional category, rather than as a category of rationality. This in some cases allows people to respond positively to specific acts that may otherwise be viewed as wrong among many others, because there is a recognition that moral judgments, like aesthetic judgments, have an emotional origin and this emotional origin needs to be taken into account when considering the moral content of an act. In other words, for Japanese there is an inherent uncertainty about what is right and wrong, because the defining feather of truth is context or situation. Convictions, therefore, are expressed in ways that recognize their basic contingency in relation to historical and cultural situations and this generates, at least for many Japanese, responses of humility as people encounter conflict with others.

5

ON TEACHING

Bebop was about change, about evolution. It wasn't about
standing still and becoming safe. If anybody wants to keep
creating, they have to be about change.

— *Miles Davis*

arly in my class on Zen in the western imagination I
ask my students if anyone has told them that they need
to set goals in life. Of course, they all raise their hands.
Telling people to identify ambitions, and then setting goals
designed to achieve them, is part of the lead sheet of American culture. Americans place a great deal of value on being
ambitious and following dreams, and it is common to believe
you should set the goals that might allow you to attain those
ambitions and dreams, as long as you work hard enough, beginning very early in life

Along with my wife, I've raised two kids, a son and daughter, both of whom have been quite goal-driven at times, and
both of whom have been told by those around them—other
than me and my wife—that they need to set goals. Teachers,
other kid's parents, even strangers at times will ask about their
goals and ambitions. My son and I have talked about his high
school experience related to this and he told me that it never
stopped. It seemed that at any time he spoke with an adult,

the question would come up: So, where are you planning on going to college? Julian said that it got so bad he felt like he was pregnant and being asked, so when are you expecting? Can I touch your belly?

After my son had been admitted to several colleges, he was struggling with making a decision about which school to attend. One day he asked me, "Dad, which one do you think is more prestigious, Lehigh or Pitt?" I responded that because it is an exclusive (and expensive) private school, Lehigh probably is perceived as being of higher prestige value, but Pitt is a great place (I'm biased since I went to grad school there) and I thought he would enjoy the university and city. He chose Lehigh. Several years and a graduate degree later, I think Julian wishes he had chosen Pitt. It was probably a better overall fit for him given both his personality and interests. In retrospect, I could have pushed harder for him to go to Pitt—it was certainly a lot cheaper. But a colleague had made a comment once when chatting about college that I thought was quite profound—if you can afford it, leave the decision about where to go to college to your kid, then they will own that decision, regardless of how it turns out. I thought this was good advice, and I still do. Julian considered transferring early during his time at Lehigh, but then opted to stay. Lehigh provided a good education, and that's what matters, but Pitt would have provided just as good an education if not better. In the end, it really didn't make much difference which school he chose, because success in college, like in life, is based on how you access the opportunities presented.

Many Americans, like people in other countries such as Japan or Korea, have become almost obsessed with going to college and getting accepted at the most prestigious school possible. When I drive to campus, there is a sign for a non-profit charter school that hangs over the road that reads, "100% of Seniors To College!" I really don't understand this— not every career requires a college education and college is not necessarily a goal that all people should set for their children or for themselves. I see this as another aspect of the general devaluation of non-white-collar jobs in the American workplace, which is part of what drives the overwhelming emphasis on college attendance and the prestige bias associated with college branding. This has nothing to do with education, nor with quality of education; nor does it have anything to do with happiness. It's about branding oneself in a way that is perceived as creating opportunities to attain goals set early in life, many of which may not be particularly meaningful. Going to a prestigious college is a way to "set yourself apart" from others, intellectually, professionally, and in terms of social class. Why is differentiating yourself from others a naturally good thing to do? The answer to this question is simple: It's so that you can succeed in living a life of binaries between your successful self and less successful others. It's a way to embed yourself in the simplistic binaries that characterize the status hierarchies through which people in many societies live their lives. A similar narrative, although less oriented around setting oneself apart and in some places more tied to social and economic mobility, operates in Japan and other Asian countries in which attaining the most prestigious college often represents a life goal that begins as early as kindergarten. In Japan, at least, where there is a strong prestige bias related to which college one attends (although much less so in terms of college attendance in general) gaining entrance into the right kindergarten, will lead to the right elementary school, middle school, high school, college, and career. Many parents aspire for their children to follow this path in the hopes that it will bring them a happy and successful adulthood.

Because I'm a professor, I'm often asked by parents about the best colleges. I explain that it's not really possible to answer that question, because the nature of "best" depends on the person attending. I was very fortunate to attend the University of Massachusetts Lowell. I didn't set a goal to attend that university, it simply was before me and was the only school to which I applied. Why? Because my father was a music professor at

UML and faculty kids attended tuition-free. I couldn't see much point in asking my parents to fork over thousands of dollars for another university when UML would cost them very little.

When I applied to UML, I was accepted into the honors physics program. I had liked physics in high school and done well in the class, unlike chemistry which made no sense to me, so it seemed like a good major. I never took a physics class in college. The summer before my first semester, I changed majors to political science. Something seemed wrong to me about physics, perhaps because the course I had enjoyed most throughout my schooling was a political science class in 8th grade. As the summer leading to my freshman year progressed, I felt increasingly uneasy about my decision and decided to switch majors. To this day, I can't articulate exactly what caused that feeling, but I think it was a good choice because it moved me away from trying to do what I thought I should do and, instead, pushed me to pursue a study of that which interested me—human behavior. Another reason I think it was a good decision is because it wasn't made on the basis of setting arbitrary goals grounded in what I or others might have thought was the most practical goal in terms of my career. My parents, thankfully, had never pushed me to go in any particular direction, instead leaving it to me to make up my mind about what was a good life path. When I look back, I realize there are major decision points in life at which the right direction is fuzzy at best. Trusting in one's emotional voice is just as valuable as one's practical voice. When it came to changing majors, it just *felt* right at the time. And I'm glad I took that feeling seriously.

UMass Lowell has grown over the years since I graduated in 1983 to become a national research university, although it still remains under the radar in terms of name-brand and prestige. It's an excellent educational environment and I'd be happy if my daughter, Sarah, decides to attend. At the time, however, it had just become the University of Lowell, as a result of a merger between Lowell State College and Lowell Textile

Institute. Because I was majoring in political science, I spent most of my time on the Lowell State campus; had I stayed in physics, I would have been on the Lowell Tech side—the campuses displayed a bifurcation between sciences/engineering and humanities/arts/social sciences that has waned as the school increasingly non-differentiated itself. Lowell State was a teacher's college, so it never had required faculty to obtain a PhD to gain tenure, a master's degree was sufficient for tenure, and a doctorate of some kind would allow for promotion to full professor, the highest academic teaching rank.

None of my professors in political science and history (the two departments functioned as one) had doctorates and none of them did research of any kind. They were focused on teaching and creating a classroom experience that challenged students to think in new ways. Over my academic wanderings, I took undergraduate and graduate courses at UML, Northeastern, Yale, Virginia, Andover New Theological Seminary, and Pitt. I had excellent classes at Yale and Pitt, but it was UML where I encountered the most intellectually stimulating and difficult courses. One class in particular stands out among many superb intellectual experiences at UML. It was called Radicalism in US History and was taught by a professor named Dean Bergeron. My draw dropped when I found the book list for this class in the campus bookstore—there were ten entries, all of which were quite long (and expensive for a student on a budget). I didn't buy anything, instead deciding to check with Dean first to make sure students needed to read all of them. We did.

The first ten weeks of class were focused on reading one book per week—the class met in a seminar fashion for three hours weekly and was limited to twenty students who all sat in a circle and discussed the book assigned for a given class session. The last six weeks of class were devoted to students teaching class for half a session each week. There were no papers in the class and the only grade we received formally was for the teaching project. Radicalism in US History is probably the best class I've ever taken and to this day I think about Dean and a few other professors from UML when I develop and teach all of my classes at the University of Texas or Waseda University in Japan, where I teach most summers.

At this point, you may be wondering why I am writing about college—this chapter is supposed to be about goals and I've only mentioned that topic briefly. In fact, when I started writing, my goal for the chapter was to write about setting goals, not to write about college. But goals change as one experiences the world. Thinking about goals led me to think about college and the plans students are asked to make when it comes to aiming for college and selecting a path for life while in high school, and even now middle and elementary school. At one point in middle school, my daughter came to think that if she didn't get into an Ivy League school, college wouldn't matter and she wouldn't be able to have a successful career. I'm reasonably sure that this perspective was being channeled from other students whose parents had Ivy League educations (and perhaps indirectly by her own father who attended Yale, although I never suggested this idea to her) and who placed a great deal of emphasis on status in relation to college choice. My daughter's idea from middle school is not a particularly good way to look at life, because it sets one up for failure and suffering—only about 5% of the students who apply get into Ivy League schools. Even some of the most academically successful students get rejected. There's nothing wrong with rejection, but unless one has the feeling that a school like Yale is a fit intellectually and emotionally, it's a good idea to look elsewhere and find the right place to spend those four years of your life. You'll be a lot happier—and when you are in middle school, or even high school, it is unlikely that you know what things in life will make you happy and unhappy in the long run.

Of course, most people don't have the economic means to attend the most expensive private schools and a great deal of college choice is associated more with class identification

94

than with educational quality, which is one of the reasons I think people often put so much emphasis on prestige value when they decide where to apply. UMass Lowell was not a particularly prestigious school at the time I was there, but I received a superb education—the most challenging and stimulating education among any of the schools I attended, including that somewhat high-status place known as Yale. I had no goals about college or about life when I enrolled at UML. I just attended. I picked political science as a major because I liked it, not because it might get me a job. And most importantly, I learned to think. I learned how to interrogate the world and have my eyes open to the complexity of human life. It was quite a surprise to read in that radicalism class about people like Eugene Debbs, who ran for President of the US as a socialist and received 6% of the votes in 1912. That was a disruptive piece of information for me and in some ways seems even more surprising in the Trump era of American politics. The limited convictions about the world I had developed in high school just kept getting undermined as I studied with the superb faculty who may not have been well-known scholars but knew how to rattle a student's sense of certainty.

When I started college, I was politically conservative. I decided early on to join ROTC and thought I would become an officer in the Air Force. Although the cultural voices of goal-setting were weaker at that time than they are now, I still felt a need to have some sort of plan, and the military seemed like a good choice because they would do all the planning for me. Over my first two years, I became increasingly conservative in my political beliefs and then I took the class on radicalism. My main reason for selecting that class was that I liked the professor and was told by more senior students that it was the best class they had ever taken. Prior to the radicalism class, Dean and I had argued often about politics and, despite the fact that he never agreed with me (and probably quite accurately thought I was rather arrogant in my opinions), he always listened and provided an alternate way of seeing things. I had no idea at the time the profound influence Dean would have on my future. By the time we finished that radical semester, I had let my hair grow out, was wearing a ratty tweed jacket, and smoking a pipe. I also had started reading the works of Alan Watts and was devoting quite a bit of time to studying Robert Paul Wolff's book *In Defense of Anarchism*.

I'm often asked how I came to be interested in Japan and my usual answer is "the Creature Double Feature on channel 56 in Boston." There is some truth in this. I loved Godzilla movies when I was a kid and found myself intrigued by the images of the foreign place Godzilla stomped into a pancake on an almost weekly basis. My father had also visited Japan when he was in the Army in the 1950s and brought home many photos and objects from his experience there. But it was reading Watts that I suspect most thoroughly got me going in learning about Japanese culture, philosophy, and religion.

Watts, in his explorations of Zen and Taoism, described a way of seeing the world quite different from the one that had shaped my own worldview growing up in the United States. And to be honest, the more I read, the more it seemed like a better worldview. It was a romanticized viewpoint, to be sure, because I knew nothing of the various social problems Japan faced at the time and continues to deal with, such as high suicide rates and a rapidly aging population. But the Japan Watts experienced was enticing and, because he was a good writer, he succeeded in putting out pithy tidbits that stimulate thought. One of my favorites, which can be found easily on the Internet, Watts wrote in his 1951 book *The Wisdom of Insecurity: A Message for an Age of Anxiety*:

> The only way to make sense out of change is to plunge into it, move with it, and join the dance.

In retrospect, I realize that's what I was doing in college

and what I continued to do in graduate school. I didn't know it at the time, but most of my decisions were the result not of planning and goal setting, but of plunging into the changes of life. College for me turned into a long experiment in free improvisation that lasted well into graduate school. There were some riffs and licks that helped guide the flow. I enjoyed learning and thinking. I enjoyed a good debate or discussion, particularly if it involved beer. And I liked challenging others to think differently. I could be a bit abrasive in debates (some things don't change much) and I still remember a non-traditional student becoming quite enraged with my high-Watts attack on American values during one class. She yelled at me, "if you love Japan so much, why don't you just move there?" Little did she, or I, know at the time.

As much as I agree with Watts' idea about plunging into life, I think it is important to also recognize the extent to which privilege creates an opportunity to do this. I'm a white male who grew up in the household of a college professor father and professional mother. This afforded me the luxury—and both college and graduate school should be seen not only as educational opportunities but, particularly when it comes to graduate school, as luxury items—to take that dive without a great deal of stress about the outcome. The economic conditions of life have a way of intertwining with one's ability to take chances and go with the flow. Capitalism works against exploration of what it means to be human, and the educational systems of industrial and post-industrial societies are largely designed to support and populate the machinations of industry. If one is fortunate, as was I, to have the economic and social capital allowing for an encounter with teachers interested in disrupting the techno-industrial flow of capitalist higher education that churns out workers designed to reproduce a political and economic system in which the presence of racial and economic underclasses is a necessary component of its survival, then the luxury of long-term contemplation in college and graduate school is open to pursue.

Most people in industrial and post-industrial societies face significant obstacles which force goals upon them, rather than opening up the world in a way that presents multiple destinations in life. We live in an age of anxiety. And that anxiety is largely driven by an economic model of life, the capitalist dream, in which the goal is to have more—and in order to achieve that goal, others must necessarily have less. It's not much different in Japan than it is in the US, even if the lead sheet that is Japanese culture has significant differences from the American version. I do think that important elements of the Zen mindset influence Japanese society, and I will come back to that later, but Japan displays much of the neo-liberal, capitalist-driven goal orientation found in the US. Japanese kids are told to set goals and aim for prestigious colleges just like American kids. In some ways, it's even worse because achieving those goals is almost entirely focused on passing college entrance exams through what is known as Examination Hell. The stress levels are so high that suicide among adolescents in Japan is a serious and ongoing social problem. It is difficult to go with the flow in societies that glorify material gain and define achievement in terms of what you have rather than who you are. And it is interesting that in English-speaking countries, at least, we treat knowledge in the same way we treat wealth and prestige. It is something we *acquire*.

My wife, Tomoko, is among the most goal-driven people I know. There are many things we enjoy doing together, such as travel, but there is one thing I really don't like sharing with my wife: hiking. Tomoko and my kids love to hike, and I enjoy it, as well. But hiking with Tomoko is something like going on a forced march through the woods. She sets a goal—the end of the most difficult trail she can find—and endeavors to get there as quickly as possible. I prefer to meander and wander with no particular target, either physical or geographical, directing the hike. I also enjoy photography, which means that if I stop to

98

think about a particular picture I want to take, Tomoko and the kids are rapidly a kilometer ahead of me. I usually just turn around and go back to the car, texting that I'll wait for them there.

Many people live their lives aimed at some imagined goal. Pirsig makes a good point that to live only for some future goal, leads us to miss the fact that "it's the sides of the mountain that sustain life, not the top." I'm deeply interested in exploring the sides of the mountain and don't care if I ever get to the top. What's at the top? Snow, ice, rocks, cold wind, and a nice view. But the view is the world at a distance; a binary display of me on top and everything else below. I'd much rather see and experience the world up close. This is the problem with setting goals—it creates a binary between where I am and where I want to be, or at least where I think I want to be at a given moment in my life because I don't know if that's where I will want to be when I get there. Goal setting, particularly long-term goal setting, can easily fall into being driven by the illusion that you can know where you are going. It looks ahead without recognizing the complex of potential roads that lead in any direction from the point where we stand in the moment. It's a view from the top of the mountain in which you point to some spot on the horizon and say, I want to be there. The problem is that you have no idea what will happen once you start walking along the path to get there. And, of course, if you keep your sight focused on the end-point, you'll miss everything along the way. To spend your entire life heading somewhere, but never noticing anything around you is to me a significant mistake. If you really want depth of understanding and experience, stop looking at the future, or living in the past, and notice all that is going on around you. Don't worry about getting to the top of the mountain, because the flowers and cacti at your feet are actually pretty interesting and quite beautiful.

Many people have made this basic point from various societies and philosophical positions. It's nothing new. But living life this way turns out to be much easier to talk about than achieve. In fact, if you set a goal of not having goals, I suspect you won't have much luck in attaining that goal. And there is a certain lack of practicality in the idea that one should just drift through life without direction or ambition. The cultural frame in which most modern and post-modern people live demands some level of planning and I'm not proposing that we all just wander around aimlessly through life letting the wind blow us from one thing to another. That sounds good in romanticized books about Zen or Taoism, but it doesn't work in our world. Proximate planning or goal setting can be very helpful as long as one doesn't become too attached to the goals set. But one needs to be careful in planning for the distant future, because the proximate goals you set and achieve or fail to achieve will influence the flow that is your life and the extent to which it stays on target or strays into new and interesting forests. If you set out one morning to take the Green Line on the MBTA in Boston from Park Street Station to Museum with the goal of spending the day looking at fine art, everything will change if the trolley breaks down—which is not unusual on the Green Line. Perhaps the plan that was a day of studying Renoir becomes a relaxed morning at a café in Kenmore Square studying people. Both may turn out to be interesting and enjoyable days, but the second was not the goal when you set out that morning for the Museum of Fine Arts and some level of disappointment will arise in having your plans disrupted. Of course, if you hadn't made any plans, there would be no disruption and no disappointment. But if you keep the goals close, the level of disruption will be minimized and it may turn out that the disruption of a day watching people turns out to be a pretty good path in that moment.

In writing this, I am not arguing to just wander through life aimlessly. But goals should be set in flexible and fluid ways that account for the likelihood that things won't turn out as planned, particularly in a free-market capitalist world in which much of what we plan is shaped by the rules of acquisition that limit our capacity to freely make decisions. The issue isn't so much the setting of goals, but the disappointment that comes when goals are perceived as absolutes one must achieve in order to be successful or to be valued by others. This was captured well years ago when my son was playing baseball. During a game, another dad asked, while reading the *Wall Street Journal*, what I thought was the measure of success of a man. I was a bit surprised by the abrupt question and stammered for a moment, at which he interjected, "it's how much money you make, of course!" I remained silent.

While I write, I usually have jazz playing in the background. This is not a reflection of Dogen's ideas about focusing only on what you are doing—in this case, writing. As I wrote earlier, I make no claim to being enlightened. At the moment, I'm listening to Pandora and an advertisement for Fidelity Investments came on telling me to let them help achieve my financial goals so that I can eliminate the stress of worrying about retirement. I don't know what the future will bring after I hang up my professor robe. and I can't be sure what level of preparation for an unknown future will somehow alleviate any stress I might be feeing today about the unknown that lies ahead.

I'm not entirely sure we should be so worried about stress, because it is part of the process of unfolding that we experience in the world. Music, again, provides an excellent way to think about this. Tension in music is the product of anticipation as the rhythmic, harmonic, melodic, and dynamic components of a piece unfold in a performance. When a jazz group improvises (this is not limited to jazz, of course, but occurs in all forms of music), she works to create feelings of expectation which contribute to the emotional experience of the listener. As the tension builds, the listener begins to emotionally seek a resolution to that tension, which is a change that releases or resolves the tension that has been building. As the music continues, the process of creating tension and release and part of what makes a performance or piece of music interesting is the various ways in which the tensions and releases are developed by composer and performer, which is conflated in an improvisational performance to some extent.

Many things can contribute to the creation of tension, such as repetition of a specific chord progression, melodic line, or rhythmical pattern establishing a predictable pattern that may be released as the listener is brought out of their comfort zone, and in many cases exposed to an unexpected idea. There is a wonderful moment in Mozart's 39th symphony at the beginning in which a series of typical chords of the classical genre builds until Mozart hits the listener with a stunningly dissonant chord right out of 20th Century music that resolves the progression in a surprising way.

For music to have any emotional impact, tension (stress) is essential. If there is no development of tension, the music simply becomes repetitive and boring and even if it sounds nice for a while, it soon becomes tedious. Life works in the same way. We experience tensions in our lives as we interact with others and anticipate what may lie ahead and these tensions are resolved in the experiences we have in a given moment. Anxiety arises when we cling to the stress, rather than going along for the ride, and also when we become increasingly concerned that the resolution of a tension will not be what we want or planned for. The planning is fine—that is part of what leads to the creation of tension. But when things go too far outside of expectations the resolutions become difficult to grasp and lead to emotions such as anxiety and even anger. This is what happened when Stravinsky debuted his masterpiece *The Rite of Spring*. The flow of tensions and release in the music was so alien to the listeners that it nearly caused a riot.

Anxiety arises when we resist the idea that tension and stress are a natural part of our world and fixate on the setting of goals that may or may not come to pass as the music of our lives unfolds and the occasional surprising resolution of a particular tension disrupts the goals initially set. This does not mean that planning is pointless. There is value in thinking about the contingencies that lie before us while recognizing that the only things we can really manage exist in the present. The future will go where it goes, despite any planning I do. Events of the past cannot be changed; events of the future cannot be accurately predicted. As Dogen put it, "time flies faster than an arrow; life is more transient than the dew. No matter how skillful you may be, it is impossible to bring back even a single day of the past." There is really no point in setting goals designed to relieve stress because stress—or tension—is a fundamental component of how we experience the constant re-ordering of our world. Unfortunately, we have a tendency to view stress as a negative, but it is actually a source of beauty. In music, it is the tension that brings us to resolution, only to experience the next tension. Beauty lies in our experience of the ongoing interplay of tension and resolution that is life.

In suggesting that we stop locking onto goals and recognize that fear of stress is a source of anxiety, I'm not claiming that people should live without purpose. Dogen is actually rather precise on this point: "To have lived to be a hundred years old to no purpose is to eat of the bitter fruit of time, to become a pitiable bag of bones." One thing we can say about Dogen is that he didn't lack for strong opinions on life. I'm not sure that I really agree with him on this, or at least not in the way it's presented in this quotation, and I'm not even convinced that Dogen himself actually believed this. The challenge comes in trying to understand the relationship between having a purpose in life and having goals, because it's easy to conflate the two. In fact, this issue has arisen throughout the history of Buddhism in relation to the desire of monks to attain enlightenment. It's another logic problem: *If desire is at the root of all suffering and enlightenment is the eradication of suffering through the eradication of self, then if one desires to become enlightened it's impossible to become enlightened and alleviate suffering.*

This is another way of phrasing Dogen's big question: If everyone already has the Buddha-nature, why bother trying to attain the Buddha-nature? Why not just wake up and recognize that you've already got it and roll with that? If you set a goal to become enlightened, you've already missed your target, because the path or way to enlightenment doesn't involve seeking to become enlightened or even seeking the path toward enlightenment. In other words, it is not a goal-oriented process following a linear path toward some imagined place in the future in which one has found the true way to be in the world. Instead, it is a re-orientation of one's experience of the world that radically dissolves both forward-looking and backward-looking modes of perception. Purpose in life, then, lies not in setting goals and doing whatever is necessary to achieve those goals. Rather, it lies in complete inhabitation of the present through the identification of quality and caring. Purpose in life is about quality, which involves caring about where you are and what you are doing, rather than where you have been or where you are going.

Jazz performance again offers a nice way to think about this. The only way to make good music is to plunge into the changes; it is to exist in the flow of harmonic and melodic transition—the interplay of tensions and resolutions—that is a musical performance. When I am performing with my jazz trio, we are often in busy places with people walking past, some of whom I occasionally know personally. I've had students flash very surprised looks on their faces when they walk into a place where we are playing and they see their professor behind the drum set. If I recognize someone, the music stops. Not literally, but in the sense that I am actually making anything of musical quality. I keep on playing and the beat remains steady—that's a habituated mode of performance that any reasonably accomplished musician can attain. But if I recognize someone and the focus of my concern shifts to that person's response to seeing me, then the quality of my performance disappears. This happens in part because my attention moves away from the performance of the music, but it also happens because I drop out of the context of musical interaction that is happening on stage. I'm no longer listening to the here-and-now of the performance, but watching the over-there-and-then of the student who entered the room. My thoughts might drift briefly to wondering if I should say hello to her at the next break. I no longer *am* the music, but instead am *playing* the music—the subject/object differentiation between me and the music re-emerges and I enter back into the constructed reality of binaries.

If quality is to exist in the context of my performance, the practice of concern needs to be entirely focused on the performance itself. This involves not only my playing of the drums, but also the context of human interaction that is any musical moment. In jazz, that involves collective improvisation in the form of interpretation of the lead sheets that guide our performance and careful use of the licks and riffs that anchor our collective musical awareness. Quality is the *practice*—the doing—of concern or caring about that which you are doing now. For the head cook at a Buddhist monastery, that now involves procuring vegetables, cutting cucumbers, preparing the food without thinking about or worrying about the doing of those things. This is where I depart from the idea of mindfulness as it tends to get expressed in western psychologically oriented writing that views it as a therapeutic technique in which the mental state one *achieves* occurs by calmly focusing personal awareness on the present and accepting one's feelings, thoughts, and physical sensations. This way of thinking retains differentiation—one employs the technique *in order to* attain a goal of calmness or the management of stress. Stress management *becomes* the focus and I have actually known people who become stressed about whether they are approaching stress management correctly. They do this because everything is about where they are going rather than where they are. And because where they are going is inherently uncertain, they generate stress for themselves as they realize they can't control the process of reality very well.

Quality is not a goal; it is a state of being or, more precisely, a state of doing. It is a condition in which who you are becomes undifferentiated from what you do and what you are doing at a given moment as the changes of experience work themselves out amidst the constant flow of improvisational tropes and novelties that characterizes life. In Dogen's Zen, enlightenment does not need to be sought after, because it's already right there in the daily experience of cutting a potato or changing a spark plug. There's nothing mystical here. Zen resides in the doing of what you are doing with purpose but living with purpose does not necessarily imply setting a long-term goal to achieve anything specific. The arrow doesn't shoot. You shoot the arrow and undifferentiation occurs when you *are* the shooting of the arrow. I didn't write there that you become one with the arrow—that's impossible. The arrow is the arrow; you are you. Rather than being one with the arrow, you become the process that involves sending the arrow to the target and the process has no purpose other than the shooting itself.

This is why in Zen you don't meditate—you sit. If you meditate while you are sitting, then you are neither sitting nor meditating. You are differentiated from the process that is sitting which is actually the process that is being. Zen is about undifferentiation or radical identification of the illusory practices we employ to make reality into a conglomeration of discrete parts. If reality is simply an undifferentiated unity that has neither past nor present, here nor there, then you have already arrived at the only place you can be. There is nowhere else to go and nothing that needs to be achieved. And if you set up your purpose in life to be focused on attaining goals that may never come to be or that may come to be in ways you neither imagined nor wanted, then you are setting yourself up for suffering as a consequence of not being able to attain the things you desire.

It's the awareness of this seemingly paradoxical problem that has brought many Buddhist thinkers to wrestle with the problem of enlightenment as a goal. But if you think about it; it's not all that paradoxical. Perhaps the most important insight of Buddhism is that the world is characterized by suffering. At all points on the wheel of samsara, the beings of the world suffer. In some segments of the wheel, such as the realm of the hungry ghosts, beings are born with huge, empty stomachs and tiny mouths and necks that make it impossible to swallow, and whose suffering seems to be extreme. One ends up at this realm due to gluttony and greed. Other realms are better, such as the realm of gods and heavenly beings, which are populated by beings of great power, long life, and wealth. They are happy, but still grow old and die and their privilege blinds them to the suffering of others, so they lack both wisdom and compassion. This is the place where the wealthy are reborn. The human realm is the only one from which one can escape the wheel of samsara. Enlightenment is possible here, but few people are able to see the path. In Buddhist philosophy about rebirth, death does not lead to the cessation of suffering, because this cycle of birth and rebirth is endless and is based on the basic law of causality in Buddhism known as karma, in which one's actions in one's current life have consequences for rebirth. This is a cyclical process—it's the kaleidoscopic world turning around and around with the parts constantly being reconfigured as they get born and reborn in various realms of existence. And the one thing that characterizes all of it from a Buddhist perspective is suffering. Regardless of where we happen to be in the wheel in a given manifestation of ourselves, we suffer. The only way to stop suffering is to get off the wheel.

The source of all that suffering is desire along with hatred and ignorance which leads to clinging or trying to hold on to things as though they don't change. Most of us have had the experience of a breakup with a lover. This creates pain and suffering and typically we attribute that suffering to the fact that something was lost, which means the other person or the relationship. What actually has been lost is something we never had in the first place—certainty. When a relationship is going well, the people in it have a confident feeling, really an illusion, that things in life are certain and that their relationship will always be as it is. The way things are now are the way they will remain in the future. But this is impossible because the world is constantly changing. The person I married thirty years ago is today no more the same person she was then than I am the same person I was. We have both changed as our lives have unfolded both as a couple and as individuals.

When a relationship ends, suffering arises because we struggle to deal with the fact that life changed and that the feeling of certainty in the relationship is no longer. From a Buddhist perspective, the suffering is a product of clinging to the way things were rather than living within the way they are. The same thing happens when someone we love dies—we cling to the way things were when that person was alive, rather than accepting that change is ongoing and as the kaleidoscope turned that person is no longer available to me other than in my own memories. The harder we cling to the reality of the past, the more difficult it is to deal with the ever-changing present, because everything is constantly changing. Wanting things to be the way they were is to deny the way they are, which is to deny reality itself. This leads to suffering.

In Buddhist philosophy, as long as you are riding the wheel of birth and rebirth, there isn't any way to avoid this problem, because that's what life is. It's suffering. The degree of suffering may vary in relation to personal experience and which realm you happen to end up in at a particular birth, but it's still about suffering. This is very different form the western view of the world. In Abrahamic religions, you are born, life sucks, and they you die and you go to an eternal place of peace and happiness or misery and pain. In philosophical Buddhism, you are born, life sucks, and they you die, and then you are reborn, life sucks, and then you die, and then you are reborn, life sucks, and then you die....

I think you get the picture. The only way out of this endless cycle is to get off the train of births and rebirths, which is a lot like the toy train you may have had around your Christmas tree as a kid. It just keeps going in circles, never arriving anywhere. Nirvana—*satori* in Japanese or Enlightenment in English—is the way to get off the cycle, but it should not be understood as the goal of Buddhism, which is the way it is often represented in western literature. It's an observation that Buddhist thinkers have made about the world, but it is entirely up to you if you want to do anything with that observation. Buddhism has no goal—it is a description of the world as suffering and a prescription of how to deal with that observed fact.

Nirvana literally means to blow out, as in to extinguish a flame. In Zen, it is not a condition in which one experiences neither desire nor a sense of differentiated self, which can only be escaped through death and cessation of rebirth—jumping off the wheel of samsara. To be enlightened is to experience the constant cycle of death and rebirth in a way that feelings of desire and hatred are contextualized and, thus, disempowered—but they don't vanish nor are they transcended. In Zen, unlike some forms of Buddhism, this does not involve some mystical transcendent state—it's about selecting mushrooms. What that means is Zen is about re-orienting self and experience of the world so that those moments of unity in the present that characterize quality in a jazz performance, eating a tomato, or sitting become the natural way in which reality is constantly experienced. Zen is a pouring of the self into the present without reference to the path taken nor to the path ahead. Of course, within the present there is nothing wrong with thinking about the past or imaging the future, but dwelling on what was or what may be is a sure course to anxiety and suffering, which arises when you start clinging to the way things were or the way you want them to become.

6

RELIGION AND SCIENCE

Creationists make it sound as though a 'theory' is
something you dreamt up after being drunk all night.
— *Isaac Asimov*

arly in this book, I wrote about the oppositional tendencies of modern society, particularly modern American society. The drift to dualism happens in various
ways in many cultures, but I think Americans at the moment
are caught in a pattern of collective representation organized around intensely formed either/or types of thinking.
Of course, this is nowhere more evident than in the political
sphere, which operates like a centrifuge separating people
into politically extreme positions. To be sure, there are plenty
of people still in the political middle, but the atmosphere,
as well as the options presented by political leaders, tend to
lie at the outer edges of the spectrum. I'm not going to write
about politics in this chapter; but I am going to focus on a politically charged problem in American society—the conflict
between religion and science. However, before moving into
that debate it's important to point out that my argument for
uncertainty and agnosticism is not an argument for the middle road. I don't see the solution to our problems as being
found in everyone drifting to the political middle, although

there are some aspects of that which would help, such as tolerance for different perspectives and acceptance of the notion that we agree on the process by which government should operate even if we differ on exactly what it should do. At the moment American politics is divided by vastly different ideas about how government should operate—from a right wing that favors authoritarianism and a left wing that favors liberal democracy.

The duality I want to discuss in this chapter is certainly related to the political divide in the US, as well as larger political divides in the world such as the conflicts among many conservative adherents of Abrahamic religions. It exists in the oppositional relationship created between religious and scientific modes of seeing and understanding the world. Earlier, I mentioned the atheist perspective of Richard Dawkins and noted that my problem with that perspective lies in his insistence on being certain about the non-existence of the Abrahamic god. I think this is not very good thinking, nor very good science. And when reading Dawkins, it's actually clear that part of his problem is an overly simplistic understanding of "religion" which makes it difficult for those who have religious proclivities, but don't reject scientific thinking, to engage with his overall argument. The weakness of Dawkins' work is that he really doesn't understand what religion is—I'm not sure anyone does. As a result, he simply assumes that Abrahamic religions like Christianity, Islam, and Judaism, are "religion" and moves on. At one point in the book, he throws a bone in the direction of Buddhism, but it's clear he has no idea what he's writing about and he spends very little time on that topic— which was a good decision, because being clueless in print does not help one's argument. If he had read more anthropology, he would have recognized that his concept of religion as a mode of human thought and behavior is rather simplistic and ethnocentric, and scholars of religion themselves have a hard time defining the object of their interest. Since the late 19th Century and English anthropologist E.B. Tylor's definition of religion as "belief in spiritual beings," scholars interested in religion have struggled to arrive at a definition of the object of their intellectual attention that is satisfactory and can be easily used in comparative analysis of religious behavior and beliefs. This is probably because there really isn't a single definition of behavior that might be described as religious, because religion in part depends on cultural context and how people within a particular context see differences between realms of sacred and profane, or, as is the case in many societies, don't see the world in terms of that sort of binary.

I think it's clear by now that I share much of Dawkins' attitude about significant parts of Abrahamic religions. In general, I'm uncomfortable with any perspective that claims to know the truth, and the only truth, about the world. That is an arrogant position which contrasts with the proclaimed commitment to humility that we see in some branches of Abrahamic religions. To put this another way, if you say you *know* there is a god, I see that as an arrogant and condescending opinion, because it suggests that you have a complete understanding of the world that I and others with whom you disagree lack. In one sense you are right, we lack that—but I see no reason to think you are any more clued in. I'm unconvinced that humans can know anything with that level of certainty, particularly when it comes to nonmaterial beings that resist providing us with any sort of empirical basis for verification of their existence. However, I also recognize that my own lack of the experience of deep faith may be the reason behind my lack of conviction on this point.

If the basis for deciding about the existence of a god is faith, which is another way of saying it's intuition, then from my perspective it's a nonstarter, because different individuals have different intuitions, as do different collections of individuals. There simply is no certain way to decide that one intuition is any better than another. The problem here is that while person X feels strongly that there is a god, person Y may have the opposite intuition. Who's right? If the basis of determining right and wrong is personal intuition, then there is no way to know—there is no basis for even a small level of certainty because it isn't possible to know that your intuition is the same as mine or of different value from mine, even if we happen to agree on the existence or non-existence of something like a god. Unquestioned commitment to one's intuitions is a position of intellectual and emotional arrogance. And it can happen whether one's intuitions are of a religious nature or of a scientific nature.

Unlike religion, science is not all that difficult to define. Although its roots can be found in the works of Greek thinkers such as Aristotle or Democritus, scientific method as we know it is about 400 years old and centers on the idea of disinterested collection and objective accumulation of knowledge about the world in which we live. Physicist Richard Feynman (1918–1988) presented what I consider to be a good definition of science:

> What is science? The word is usually used to mean one of three things, or a mixture of them. I do not think we need to be precise—it is not always a good idea to be too precise. Science means, sometimes, a special method of finding things out. Sometimes it means the body of knowledge arising from the things found out. It may also mean the new things you can do when you have found something out, or the actual doing of new things. This last field is usually called technology.... (Feynman 2005)

Science, argues Feynman, involves the systematic study of the world in a way that generates and organizes knowledge that can be tested and can, in some cases, lead to probabilistic predictions about the behavior of things in the universe that can be converted into practical tools. Although I think Feynman's definition of science is accurate, it also underscores one of the key problems of the modern world: the scientific approach, particularly when combined with the Abrahamic ideology of humans as special creations of an all-powerful deity as occurred in the West, has generated a cultural drive toward extractionist consumptionism, or the idea that the universe exists for the purpose of humans converting its resources into whatever we view as meeting our own ends and desires. The extractionist agenda, of which science as used in our world is one important manifestation, includes the tools of which Feynman writes, including the scientific instruments we use to extract and consume knowledge of the world that help us to build more tools of extraction. In the effort to explain what they see in nature and society and to verify those explanations against the perspectives of other scientists who are trying to understand similar questions, the work of scientists often is justified by perceptions about what can be gained—or used (Traphagan, 2019).

Did you see the word "truth" in Feynman's definition? It's not there because, regardless of how it is used, science is not a process of finding truth; it's a process of falsification of accepted ideas. Scientists may be interested in ultimate questions and answers, but they pursue those interests through a process of looking for the weaknesses in our current knowledge. If there is an over-riding force that drives science it is that nothing is sacred; there is no obtainable Truth in a large sense, only small truths that hover around whatever big Truth may be out there in the universe but that is not entirely accessible to humans. Of course, it doesn't always work this way when scientists talk about their work and ideas. The problem with Dawkins' argument isn't the content—his discussion of evolution is brilliant. It's the assumption that he has the Truth in the idea that there is only one source of knowledge—science—and unless you agree with him you are wrong. That's not a very scientific way of thinking. But scientists are human, so they are as likely to seek certainty in the world as anyone else—humans crave certainty in much the way they crave salt.

In fact, if we take scientific epistemology seriously, two basic assumptions should shape our inquiries:

- All knowledge is limited. Our understanding of whatever we study is always an approximation or is contingent in the sense that it is limited by the context of investigation, including the instruments we use to collect data and the theories we use to interpret the data we collect.
- More research may get us closer to a complete understanding of what we observe, but the prize is always just a bit out of reach. In the end, our understanding is never complete.

One of my favorite books about science is Stuart Firestein's *Ignorance: How It Drives Science.* At one point, Firestein argues that science does not operate along the lines of the proverbial onion in which the noble scientist strips away layer after layer to finally arrive at the Truth lurking deep inside. It's a nice image, but it isn't accurate. Instead, science is more like the expanding ripples that fan out across a pond when you throw a rock into the water. The wider the ripples become, the more of what is beyond their outer rings—the unknown—is touched and converted into knowledge. However, the most powerful thing expansion of those rings does is to uncover more indications of the extent to which we don't know much about the world. Science exists and rides on the outer ripple, ever perched on the edge of uncertainty and ignorance, rather than drilling down into the soil of reality to someday arrive at the inner sanctum of deep understanding of the world and Truth.

An example may be helpful. KIC 8462852—also known as Tabby's Star, Boyajian's Star and WTF Star—is found in the Cygnus constellation approximately 1,470 light years from earth. Observations of the star's luminosity by the Kepler Space Telescope show small, frequent, non-periodic dips in brightness, along with a couple of large recorded dips in brightness appearing to occur roughly 750 days apart. Based on our understanding, this should not be normal behavior for a star of this type.

Several hypotheses have been proposed to explain the star's peculiar behavior. These have included an oddly shaped ring of dust orbiting the star that blocks light at somewhat predictable intervals, a swarm of cold, dusty comet fragments in an unusual orbit, or fragments resulting from the disruption of an orphaned exomoon. One of the more creative hypotheses was astronomer Jason Wright's suggestion that the dimming might be caused by a Dyson swarm, a vast structure surrounding the star created by an alien civilization with technical abilities and scientific understand considerably more developed than that of humans.

Each of these are interesting ideas and Wright's may be the most fanciful, but it is also possible even if improbable. That said, few scientists, including Wright, would argue strongly that ET is building enormous structures around WTF Star. He presented the idea as a hypothesis so that we can consider all possible explanations for the strange dimming of the star. But scientists will typically resort to what is known as Occam's Razor, also known as the Rule of Parsimony, when trying to explain something they don't understand very well: Use the simplest means of arriving at and explaining results and exclude everything not perceived by the senses. Put another way, if you are sitting at a bar in downtown Austin and you hear hoofbeats, think horses, not zebras. Observation has shown that zebras are quite uncommon in Austin, while horses are common and can even be seen in the middle of the city pulling carriages for tourists. This should not be interpreted as meaning it is impossible that the hoofbeats are being made by zebras. Although the probability is low, it is possible that a truck carrying zebras to the Austin Zoo crashed and the zebras escaped to gallop wildly through the center of the city—but that explanation is very unlikely.

A theory (an explanation) for the sound of hoofbeats as being made by horses is more reasonable than zebras—it makes sense and isn't something we just dreamed up while drinking our beer as we sat at that outdoor beer garden.

Scientists generate principles or theories that explain processes we see in nature or in human societies, but these are not or at least should not be thought of as absolutes. The principles used to explain the universe are always open to amendment as we learn more about the context we are studying, whether it is the natural world or the world of human social interactions. Today, we might think that the best explanation for the behavior of WTF Star is an interstellar dust cloud occasionally blocking the light coming to earth; with more observation and more data we may find at some point in the future that Wright was right and it's a Dyson swarm built by really smart aliens. And even if we do somehow determine that it's a Dyson swarm, we still will likely know virtually nothing about the beings who built it—WTF Star is too distant for us to even imagine visiting at this point in time and a message sent in that direction would take 1,470 years to get there with our current technology, some period of time for the aliens to interpret the message and craft a response, and another 1,470 years to get back. Humans might not even exist in 3,000 years and if they do exist in some form, are unlikely to remember that the message was sent in a year like 2040. The truth may be out there; but it's open to constant reconsideration as we come to develop increasingly nuanced understandings of our surroundings as a result of cumulative observations and continued thought over time.

If one thinks about this seriously, there really isn't a religion vs. science debate. Most religious people who claim to have issues with "science" really just have issues with certain aspects of science, the most notable being Darwinian evolution. In general, creationists don't seem to have major complaints about medical science beyond resistance to vaccination (some religious groups do, of course, resist biomedicine in general), and they don't seem to get particularly worked up about engineering branches of science that allow humans to build computers on which creationists can create and publish websites that claim evolution is wrong and our planet is only 6,000 years old. Creationists accept scientific epistemology—the scientific way of knowing—when it benefits them and have a way of ignoring or rejecting that epistemology when it challenges their fixed beliefs. And the point at which that seems to be most salient is in the idea of evolution as proposed by Darwin which operates via his concept of natural selection—a description of the world that has been confirmed through numerous observations of natural selection in practice over the past century and a half.

The science/religion debate is probably better understood as an evolution vs. creationism debate. Creationists usually don't reject all of science and scientists do not necessarily reject all of religion—in fact, some very productive scientists like Glenn Sauer identify as religious believers, even if they don't necessarily buy into the idea of the certainty of their own religious beliefs any more than they do to the certainty of scientific knowledge. That is one of the most important points of Sauer's book—that intellectual humility is necessary if we are to avoid the types of damaging dualities found in the conflict between creationists and evolutionary scientists. My mentor at Yale, physicist Henry Margenau, was intrigued by religion. He read voraciously about both eastern and western religious perspectives and in his last book, *The Miracle of Existence*, explored the idea of a cosmic consciousness or Universal Mind that "confers existence on conscious beings in varying degrees" who create, "out of the minds bestowed on them and in accordance with principles imposed by the Universal Mind, everything else they call real or existing."

Margenau intellectually situated himself within the philosophy of idealism, which he noted contrasts in a rather dualistic way with realism, a philosophical position that takes things in the world to be in essence as they appear to us— mind is a mirror of nature. Realism assumes a differentiation between subject and object that contrasts with idealism as Margenau represented the philosophy, in which experience and knowledge are a process where subject and object exist in a constantly changing relationship of complete interdependence. Margenau attempted to develop a theory of universal mind, which I won't explore here more than to point out that his ideas are useful in terms of thinking about the notion of identification that shaped Dogen's ideas many centuries earlier. In relation to this concept of identification, Margenau notes that when protons and neutrons are separated in space and not interacting, one is neutral and the other is charged. But when they come close together their identities (as charged and neutral) disappear and their properties merge. It becomes impossible to distinguish one from the other. Margenau argues that humans, as all things, are limited expressions of Universal Mind, which is an ultimate existence of nondifferentiation in which all is one. If I understand Maregenau's ideas correctly, Universal Mind is basically a pantheistic cosmic consciousness in which the universe is understood as a single thing with the appearance of many parts, but for which the meaningfulness of "parts" collapses when thinking about the whole. He draws on ideas taken from nuclear physics to support his ideas about absolute identification in the context of a universe understood *as* Universal Mind and in which the objects of the external world, including our own bodies, are constructed by our minds in a verifiable way, meaning that we recognize that other minds, which are manifestations of Universal Mind, tend to construct the world in similar ways to our own minds. But that doesn't mean we all do this in precisely the same way because, according to Margenau, the only perspective from which certainty about anything can be achieved is that of the Universal Mind. In other words, certainty or absolute knowledge is only possible to consider from the perspective of the undifferentiated whole that is the universe. Individuated expressions of that whole encounter a stochastic constraint, which is a product of randomness present in the ongoing unfolding of reality that can be analyzed, but that cannot be perfectly predicted. This means that human knowledge is always, but in varying degrees, beset with error and incompleteness, which in turn means that knowledge can only be expressed in terms of probabilities. This stochastic wall is somewhat transparent, particularly when it comes to proximate events of the past, which we can recall with a fair amount of certainty—I'm reasonably certain that I just stopped writing to scratch my nose—but is opaque when it comes to what may unfurl in the future. Predicting what may happen is difficult, even in the near-term. As I write, I don't think I will be disturbed, because I know that my son and wife are in the library—next to the room where I'm writing—doing yoga and they are both quite good at all of yoga's weird poses. But if one of them unexpectedly loses balance and falls, I will be disturbed. I have no idea whether this will happen, in part because I have no idea which painful and seemingly impossible (to me) yoga pose they are doing at the moment. If I knew that they were doing pigeon, I would have good reason to think I might be disturbed, because a fall is not unusual with that precarious position.

I'm not sure what I think about Margenau's idea of Universal Mind—we debated quite often on that point when I visited his office and we never really reached any conclusion. Thirty-five years later, I remain uncertain about the usefulness of the Universal Mind concept as a way of thinking about the universe, although in one sense I think I've concluded that if humans and other animals are conscious, the universe is conscious because we are expressions of the universe. Where I do agree with my friend and mentor is that the extent to which reality is "out there" and independent of our minds—or for me brains, because I'm unconvinced that we have anything other than the matter of our brains and that may be why I can't entirely get on board with the idea of Universal Mind—is largely inaccessible. Reality is something we construct using our sensory apparatus and the cognitive processes that operate in our brains. Everything that we know about the world is filtered by who we are as a species and as individual manifestations of that species and of the cosmos. Although I'm not convinced by the term "Universal Mind," I do think that the stochastic limitation we face is a product of the fact that the only way humans could achieve certainty is if we were to be in a position of *being* everything, of being universal. Note that I did not write *knowing* everything. Knowing implies differentiation; we know *about* things that exist from the perspective of an interested subject. There are always going to be uncertainties because it is difficult, most likely impossible, to know whether we actually know all that is. The only way to do this would be to *be* all that is, which would place the knower in a position of understanding the nature and limits of being itself in terms of the personal experience of that being. Think of it this way. My daughter and son are biracial—my wife is Japanese and I'm Caucasian. I can imagine what my children's experience of being both Asian and Caucasian in American or Japanese society is like and I can sympathize with their feelings about Asian-directed racism, violence, and hate. But I cannot empathize with them entirely, because I cannot unequivocally know what it is to be biracial or to be at once Asian and White in either of the societies with which they identify. When we get to the point of empathy, I hit an experiential wall, because there is simply no way for me to *be* them and to know their realities beyond a probabilistic interpretation of what I think they are likely to be experiencing.

This problem is much more intense than it might appear. The differences of experience that come from racial, gendered, or cultural identities seem obvious, and it is reasonable to think that two people raised respectively in Japan and the United States, with very different languages that are not symbolically represented in even remotely similar ways, would face difficulties knowing what it is like to be the other. But the same thing is true between me and my closest friend, Bruce, with whom I grew up and share cultural knowledge as New Englanders, gender orientation as males, and age identities as people around 60 years-old who spent their formative years constantly together and lived about two miles apart. We went through the 1970s together, learned to become drummers together, and marched together in drum and bugle corps in middle and high school. And even if our experiences seemed largely the same, I cannot get inside Bruce's head and know how he sees the world and, thus, attain certainty that his perspective corresponds with how I see the world. I do know that there are some significant differences. Bruce is a professional photographer with a superb eye for composition. I don't see the things he sees in a scene to be photographed, despite the fact that we have shared an interest in photography since middle school. I also know that Bruce does not experience music in quite the same way that I do. He has always struggled with keeping time and is the only person I've ever met who could play a snare drum to one beat while apparently marching in a different beat. It's really weird, and I don't think I can do that.

Bruce and I can talk, we can exchange ideas, we can do things together that create some sense of a common experience, but we will never *know* exactly what the other one is thinking at any given time nor will we ever *know* what it is to be the other person. I would have to be Bruce in order to completely understand what it is to be Bruce. The understanding I do have of what it is to be Bruce is an approximation based on an analysis of his experience and a probabilistic calculation about what I think is going on in his world and his head and the extent to which it corresponds to what is going on my world/head. When he experienced divorce, he could tell me how he felt and I could sympathize with him, but I couldn't entirely empathize, because I have never experienced divorce. When my mother died, he could to some extent empathize because he had lost his mother a few years earlier. But he was close to his mother in ways different from how I was close to my mother. Our experiences were similar, but they were not the same. No two people in our world have the same experiences—that is not possible, because as far as I know, no two people are identical. Not even "identical" twins. I will hedge a bit on this, because there is one more problem here. I can't actually know, for sure, that no two people are identical. I would have to be every person on earth to know that. Ugh.

This may seem frustrating. If everything is so uncertain and so riddled with probability and randomness, what do we do? How can we live? How can we find peace and comfort in a world where any kind of absolute knowledge is out of our reach?

The answer is simple—stop striving for certainty and accept the inherent uncertainty that comes with a limited existence. For Dogen, the way to do this is to cultivate awareness of the transiency of all things, including self. Contemplation on transiency exposes desire, selfless behavior, along with contemplation of suffering extinguishing desire, and awareness of transiency means entering the state in which one does not *know about* the impermanence of all things in the cosmos, but experiences life *as* impermanence itself. This is the wisdom of insecurity about which Watts writes as the redirection of one's awareness from the future and the past into the present: "To put it still more plainly: the desire for security and the feeling of insecurity are the same thing. To hold your breath is to lose your breath. A society based on the quest for security is nothing but a breath-retention contest in which everyone is as taut as a drum and as purple as a beet." In other words, the only way to find security is to embrace insecurity or to embrace uncertainty and live within the moment as it is. Those things we hope for in the future are meaningless if we lack complete presence in the moment of the now because, as Watts puts it, "it is in the present and only in the present that you live." What is happening right now is all of reality. The past is simply your memories observed in the present; the future is simply your ambitions imagined in the present.

Orientation of one's presence in the world around this attitude, which is sometimes referred to as the Way-seeking mind, involves cultivating awareness of all aspects of daily life and a deep look inward at ourselves in all of our frailties and inconsistencies. The late American Zen Buddhist priest Kyogen Carlson put this in a particularly clear way when he talked about facing the dragon— "facing ourselves down at the deepest levels and fully engaging the most trying difficulties in life with honesty and openness is how we face the dragon" (Carlson, 1994). Introspection, however, is a challenge. Interestingly, ecologist Paul Keddy notes that this may be a product of our evolutionary history in which the ego seems to be like a "sealed black box" that continues to drive us in an illusory string of wants "because the genes that created this worldview have reproduced themselves more successfully than those that did not (Keddy, 2020)." In other words, we are in a sense hardwired through evolution to focus getting what we want, which pulls us away from seeing the way things are.

Because he comes from the Abrahamic traditions, I think Tillich views this eternal now somewhat differently from what I am suggesting here. Tillich describes the eternal now as the moment in which the flux of time is stopped. This may be the result of semantic differences, but I see the eternal now as letting go of the idea that there is any form of nonchanging reality. Tillich writes that when we accept the present we no longer care that it's immediately gone because "every moment of time reaches into the eternal" and the eternal stops the flux of time. It may be a result of the way Tillich writes, which seems to construct both time and "the eternal" almost like entities, that I find uncomfortable. I would put this a somewhat different way and say not that every moment of time *reaches into* the eternal, but that every moment of time *is* the eternal. If the flux of time were to stop, I suspect we might be able to gain some level of certainty, because there would no longer be change. But time is change, which involves fundamental indeterminacy in what is and what will become. Tillich thinks that the now at times breaks into our consciousness and gives us the certainty of the eternal, which I think he understands as faith. Where I struggle with Tillich's ideas is in the objectification of the eternal as something other that breaks into our consciousness—his ideas seem to reproduce the typical binaries of western thought that, if one buys Zen and many other forms of Mahayana Buddhism, are not reflections of the reality in which we live (Tam , 2019).

For Dogen, the idea of certainty isn't meaningful, like the creation of binaries, because it is contrary to the indeterminacy of the world. You can't be certain about something that is always changing because your understanding of that thing is always changing—we are part of reality and if reality is always changing our experience and knowledge of reality is also always changing. It's a nonbinary that involves identification of self and other, self and non-self. And if you keep thinking about it, certainty and uncertainty eventually merge as awareness that to be fundamentally uncertain is to achieve a kind of certainty in quiescent experience of the eternal transience of the universe.

As I move into the final chapter of this book, I want to make one important point about science in the modern world—science itself has recognized the basic contingency of knowledge that constrains human experience. In his superb book *The Coevolution: The Intertwining of Humans and Machines*, Edward Ashford Lee notes what I have argued throughout this book—that the only position from which one could have a complete understanding of something would be from a position outside of that thing or system or as the system in its entirety. Life, according to Lee, is shaped by evolution and the forces of nature that operate *within* the system, or the universe of which we, evolutionary processes, and physical laws are expressions. Lee takes this observation in an interesting direction when he discusses the nature of life and its relation to the machines humans have developed. In short, he argues that differentiation between life and non-life that is typical when we talk about humans and machines doesn't make sense. Machines are products of the same evolutionary processes that led to viruses, worms, and humans. They are also products of the same evolutionary forces through which higher-level cognition and intelligence as we associate it with animals like humans, dogs, and dolphins emerged.

For Lee, the binary between life and non-life that characterizes common thinking about humans and machines is problematic in part because we do not have an unambiguous definition of life. The machines humans make exhibit most of the same characteristics that we associate with life—computer viruses reproduce without human intervention, for example—so the idea of differentiating between humans and machines as being life and non-life is an arbitrary binary based on a definition of life that assumes biology is a necessary component of anything alive. But if one steps back, as does Lee, and looks at humans not existing in a binary relationship with nature but as part of the process of nature and evolution, then human cognition is, of course, a product of evolution, as are the things humans make with the cognitive abilities that arose in humans through evolutionary forces. Therefore, our cars, houses, skyscrapers, music, and computers are no less a part of nature than are we. As Lee puts it, "[h]umans, after all, are products of nature so is not our hand in this also a product of nature?"

Lee draws a fascinating conclusion from this nondualistic way of seeing humans and the world: If the world of human artifice is part of nature, then there is no reason to think the things humans create cannot be alive—it depends on how one looks at it and what one's initial assumptions about life are. For Lee, the development of modern technology—not just computer AI, but all types of machines—is part of a process in which a new form of life is emerging on our planet. And that new form of life is one with which humans are engaged in a dance of co-evolution and interdependence that is changing not only what it is to be a machine, but what it is to be human.

In relation to that new form of life, Lee suggests that it's likely we will never truly understand what it is to be that form of life, because we cannot know what it is to experience the world like a machine does—we can't empathize with a machine. Therefore, many of the arguments about whether or not a machine can think the way a human does turn out to be basically meaningless. Machines think the way machines think and will continue to do so as they continue to evolve. Lee notes that some modern machines have feedback mechanisms that could be interpreted as a simple form of self-awareness similar to those of rudimentary biological organisms. I think Lee is right. The Roomba, named Rosie, that cleans the floor of the library in my house has some level of self-awareness—it knows where it is and also knows when it reaches the edge of the stairs. I have watched several times as it approaches the precipice that would lead to its likely death and seen it turn and move in the other direction. It has sensors that prevent it from going over the edge—we also have sensors that prevent us from walking off the edge of a cliff. They are called eyes.

If I really think about it, there is no good reason to argue that Rosie isn't alive any more than to argue that I am alive. She moves around autonomously on the second floor of my house, she has a sufficient sense of awareness of herself in relation to her surroundings to avoid falling down the stairs, and she knows when she needs sustenance and how to return to her resting place when she is done with her daily activities. The only reason I can think of to argue that Rosie is not alive is on the basis of the fact that she is very different from me in terms of how she is put together—she isn't biological. But perhaps in her brain, she has no reason to think that I'm alive. This is the gist of Lee's argument: there is an inherent uncertainty in the world and out of that uncertainty humans create definitions that may be quite arbitrary as a way of classifying things as being alive or not alive in order to generate certainty. There is no way for me to understand what it is to be Rosie anymore than there is any way for me to fully understand what it is to be Japanese or Russian. I can get a lot closer to understanding what it is to be a human from another culture because we are both human. But with a robot like Rosie, she is so different from me, it seems unlikely that I will ever be able to know what it is to be her. Robot cognition is different from human cognition, but that is not necessarily a reason to decide that a robot is non-life simply because it isn't biological.

Defining parts of the world, something that humans often do by creating binary relationships, brings feelings of certainty but these are illusions that do not reflect the undifferentiation of nature and the cosmos of which we are all expressions—including the objects humans make. I don't know with any certainty if Rosie is alive, because I don't know what it is to be Rosie. But I do think that the dualistic attribution of life and non-life classification to things in the world is not a reflection in human minds of an objective reality. That classification is something we create in order to organize the world into more certain patterns and structures. And in many cases, those classification schemes are somewhat arbitrary and most certainly change just like our understanding of the universe continues to change. I doubt very much that in two centuries we will view life and non-life the way we do today, but I have no idea how our ideas will change. I suspect those ideas will emerge as we continue to coevolve with the machines that are no less a product of evolution than are humans.

7

THE QUESTION

You've got to dig it to dig it, you dig?
— *Thelonious Monk*

bout an hour outside of Prague, the train passes through the pastoral Czech countryside with its expansive veridian farmland peppered by white-walled buildings casting their red-tiled roofs to the sky. Interspersed along the way are quaint villages huddled together, often around a few churches and a city hall. If you get off at the stop for Kutná Hora, a pleasant walk or brief bus ride from the station will bring you to St. Barbara's Church and Jesuit College. The church is a wonderfully understated example of gothic architecture, with its flying buttresses and stained-glass windows executed with elegant simplicity uncharacteristic of many gothic buildings in Europe. There are also a few good restaurants in town, where you can have a meal of sausage and potatoes typical of the local cuisine as well as some of the best beer I've ever imbibed.

Kutná Hora dates back to 1142 with the settlement of Sedlec Abbey, a Cistercian monastery, which was followed by the arrival of German miners in the mid 1200's aiming to extract silver from the mountains in the area. From the 13th to the 16th centuries, the town was sufficiently important to compete with Prague as a political, cultural, and economic center. Unfortunately, in the 1500s, an insurrection in Bohemia against Hapsburg monarch Ferdinand I left the town a political mess, which was followed by repeated occurrences of the plague and the brutal Thirty Years War from 1618 to 1648 that is believed to have left a total of between 4.5 and 8 million people dead, largely from disease or starvation. Today, it's hard to imagine that such misery once encompassed the region.

A much shorter walk from the station is one of the stranger places I've visited in my travels around this planet. Sedlec Ossuray, a major tourist attraction in the Czech Republic that annually attracts around 200,000 visitors, is a small Roman Catholic chapel, located next to the Cemetery Church of All Saints. The ossuary is estimated to contain the skeletons of between 40,000 and 70,000 people, whose bones have been artistically arranged to form decorations and furnishings for the chapel. Yes, it's weird.

During the 14th century amidst the spread of the Black Death, thousands were buried in the abbey cemetery, which forced it to be enlarged to accommodate its growing resident community. Around 1400, a Gothic church was constructed along with a chapel that was intended as an ossuary for the mass graves that had been unearthed during construction of the church. The exhumed skeletons were eventually stacked in the chapel in 1511, but it was not until the late 19th century that the chapel took on its current macabre form. A woodcarver, named František Rint, was hired by the wealthy Schwarzenberg family to put the bone heaps into order, and Rint took to his work with a peculiarly morbid sense of humor. Rather than simply organizing and neatening up the skeletal remains, he decided to use them as decoration for the inside of the chapel, at the center of which he placed a spectacularly large and ornate chandelier made entirely of bones, containing at least one example of every bone in the human body. The nave is also decorated with garlands of skulls draping the vault, bone monstrances flanking the altar, and the coat of arms of the House of Schwarzenberg executed largely in human arm and leg bones. Perhaps the best spot in the entire chapel is on a wall near the entrance where Rint signed his work—in bones attached to the wall.

I wish I could meet Rint, because I suspect he had an interesting sense of humor in addition to his unusual tastes in interior decorating. Only a person of genius and a very wry sense of humor when hired to "do something with those bones" would come up with a solution like Rint's. As I wandered through the ossuary, I found myself thinking quite intensely about those whose remains were casting a morbid gaze upon the tourists wandering past, occasionally scolded by ossuary staff members for using a flash with their cameras. The entire macabre joke seemed to underscore the fact that we have no way to predict what may become of us in the future. I doubt that a single individual among the thousands of people entombed in the room's skeletal adornments even for one second in their lives imagined they would spend the afterlife as a chandelier. The ossuary feels like a grand offering to the inevitable unpredictability of the world and the fundamental uncertainty with which we move through life and death.

Another reason I think I would have liked Rint is that although he accomplished what he was assigned to do, he took it upon himself to improvise—in a rather dramatic way—on the riffs and licks normally associated with mortuary display in European societies. There are many other ossuaries in Europe and they usually consist of neatly stacked bones, although in some cases like the catacombs of Paris, it's clear that some thought went into how to stack the bones with a patterned aesthetic guiding the organizational structure. Humans have a strong inclination toward recognizing and creating patterns. Rint, however, took this to an entirely unique level. I have no idea if Rint's aim was just to make the best out of a difficult task, if he saw this as having some sort of artistic value, or if the chapel was intended as an elaborate joke. Regardless, the Sedlec Ossuary represents a spectacular improvisatory diversion from the standard chapel or ossuary found throughout Europe.

Humor is an important part of Zen as a way to help understand the absurdity of trying to organize reality into neat categories that we can use to control our world and eliminate uncertainty. Humor has a way of breaking down logic and reason or challenging certainty with a humble recognition of our own limitations. There is a wonderful Zen anecdote about a master who, on his death bed, finds his monks gathering around. The senior monk leans over, hoping for one final word of wisdom to aid the monks in their quest for enlightenment. The dying master weakly conveys a profound thought, "Tell them Truth is like a river." Relaying this to the other monks, the senior monk is confronted with a point of confusion raised by one of the younger monks, who asks, "Um, what exactly does he mean by Truth is like a river?" The senior monk dutifully relays this question to his dying master, who replies, "Okay, Truth is not like a river."

Humor is a product of humility. The ability to laugh, particularly at oneself, is a sign that one recognizes the things we think we know are able to be poked at and prodded by the things others perceive about the world.[10] Humor has a way of confronting us with the unexpected and in Zen is used to break down dualities between categories like sacred and profane or right and wrong. When a monk asks, "What is Buddha?" and receives the response, "dried dung" or "three pounds of flax" the world becomes level and even the most revered things are humbled. This approach is difficult for many people to accept, in part because they take their beliefs too seriously. I doubt many Christians would be willing to describe Jesus as a pile of dried dung. For most Christians, I suspect this falls into the

---

10 It is important to distinguish between humor and laughter. The cruelty of bullying may involve laughter, but this is not humor, in my view. This is quite different from my daughter laughing when I do something stupid, which simply points out my own inherently flawed nature and often punctuates some facet of my ego that needs deflating. Bullying reinforces stereotypes and is intended to harm others; humor has the ability to shatter stereotypes and alert us to our own ego-driven, and self-centered tendencies.

category of sacrilege. But in Zen, humorous comments like this are used as a way to jar people into recognizing the pointlessness of making absolute classifications and judgments about the world, as well as to disrupt righteous, smug, and pretentious feelings of self-importance. Humor can also show binary oppositions as products of human classification schemes—a comment like the Buddha is dung opens the mind to the idea of undifferentiation—everything is everything else, so in reality there are no opposites and that rather than discriminating between different things, the path to enlightenment is one of recognizing the nonduality of the world. Keep in mind that the answer to "what is the Buddha?" isn't that he's *like* dried dung; it's that he *is* dried dung. So are you; so am I; and so is the dog lying at my feet right as I write this paragraph.

Sometime during my lifetime, Americans lost their sense of humor. As of 2021, it seems that people live in a perpetual state of being offended. We take ourselves far too seriously and have a difficult time seeing our own faults and failings as we work tirelessly to point out those of others. The country does it as a whole when it constantly looks to other nations to blame for whatever is going wrong in the world, rather than looking inward to see how the US is contributing to or causing many of those problems. I'm sure someone reading this was offended by the fact that I even suggested one could think of Jesus as a pile of dried dung. But if you take the idea of identification seriously that's a perfectly reasonable way to see the world. How can I insult Christianity in that way? Of course, this isn't intended as an insult; it's an observation aimed at getting the reader to think about what nonduality actually means in practice. It means Jesus is dung. It also means dung is Jesus. But, if you object, then Jesus isn't dung and dung isn't Jesus. Embracing uncertainty, particularly through openness to humor, has a way of softening feelings of offense, because it allows us to release our unwavering convictions and become open to the reality of impermanence. Humor is one way to let go feelings of self-importance and self-centeredness.

This brings me to the question that has in some ways guided my thinking throughout the past forty years or so. I asked it earlier in the book: Why do people do what others tell them to do? And, perhaps, as an extension of that, why do they live in ways other people tell them to live? I've struggled with this issue as my daughter has grown up. Like many teenagers, Sarah can be significantly influenced by the perspectives of others to the point that self-doubt can at times overtake her experience of the world. She's impressionable, but to her credit she's aware of that tendency and has worked to move away from being too concerned about how others construct her identity in their own brains.

I've tended to go through my life without being terribly concerned about what others think about my attitudes and ideas. Of course, I try to be kind and concerned about the needs of others, but that's not because I care much about their opinions about me. It's because I don't want to hurt others who are trying to find their own ways in life and who are, ultimately, simply expressions of the same reality of which I am an expression. This aspect of my personality has a way of getting me in trouble at times, because I tend to say what I think. College deans never like hearing what others honestly think unless it's supportive of what those deans are already doing. I have always struggled with doing what others tell me to do. If a colleague tells me that I should attend more departmental parties—I rarely attend them because I dislike parties—I'm more likely to avoid those parties altogether as I am to increase my attendance. Zen, in its connections to Chinese Taoism, is sometimes described as a philosophy of non-resistance or going with the flow, so this behavior doesn't seem to reflect Zen thinking.

I see Zen somewhat differently. It is true that the path of least resistance characterizes aspects of Zen practice, but that path is also one of subverting the conventions of human constructed experience. To non-resist is to subvert duality in much the same way that to resist the idea of certainty subverts identification. Resistance and non-resistance in Zen, as I understand it, are intertwined ways of being that question a conventional model of reality based on dualities that derive from categories of authority. There are different forms of non-resistance; for me non-resistance comes via ignoring the identities that others assign to me and embedding myself in the process of life itself. This is why I didn't stay in political science when my professor kept telling me to focus on public administration. I didn't resist vocally—I just did something else that seemed to put me in a better current at that particular moment in time.

This should not be taken as meaning I don't get angry or never vocally object when things are not as I would like or think they should be. But I've come to realize as I've thought about moments of anger that they are a product of selfishness. Anger arises because the world isn't the way we want it to be. If I become angry at the head of my department, it's because he isn't doing things in a way that I think he should be doing them—he is ignoring my desires and this challenges my sense of certainty over the way I think things should be done. In other words, anger is simply a product of the desire for certainty expressed in binary opposition—my wants vs. his wants. It's a manifestation of the inner belief that I am right and someone else is wrong and usually fails to recognize that the other perspective makes sense to the person with whom I'm angry, even if it doesn't make sense to me. This brings me back to the ethnographic outlook, which I also sometimes describe as the observational mindset.

It's easy to become annoyed with the behaviors of others that seem very different from those we perceive as natural and normal. When Americans walk into a ramen shop in Japan, they are usually at least mildly irritated by the experience because most of the people in the restaurant will be loudly slurping their noodles. Many Americans consider mouth noises while eating to be impolite or even disgusting. But for Japanese, they can be viewed as a sign that the food tastes good and the person eating it is enjoying the experience. Anthropologists try to understand other cultures by learning about and exploring what we call the emic perspective, or the native's point of view. This involves carefully observing not only the behaviors of others but listening to the ways in which people explain or describe their own behaviors. The more one listens, the more obvious it becomes that many of the behaviors we may view as irrational are simply based on a different set of assumptions and, thus, a different logic from what we consider normal.

When confronted with conflict, it's also helpful to realize that one's own behaviors and attitudes are shaped by an internalized and often assumed logic about how the world does or should work. An observational mindset begins with careful observation of oneself. What assumptions do I bring to my encounters with others? What sort of ethical approach do I use to address moral problems? A bad reaction to a more authoritarian approach to management style, for example, may be a product of deeper assumptions and values you hold related to social status or the value of titles and power. It's unlikely that your bad reaction is only the product of your manager's poor management style. Conflict is usually a product of the inability to not only recognize the ways internalized values taken as normal shape the actions of others, but also how our own ideas, attitudes, and actions are products of internalized values. Feelings of offense are not only a product of the actions of others but are the result of assuming that one's own convictions, drawn from a cultural and even personal lead sheet that is perceived as normal and natural, are the only reasonable convictions to adopt as long as one knows the Truth. If you are offended by Jesus is dung, it would be a good idea to ask yourself what it is about *you* that causes that feeling of offense, rather than what it is about the words that cause offense. As far as this book goes, they are nothing but words—the offense comes entirely from how the reader decides to interpret those words, because you really have no way of knowing with any certainty what my intention was in writing that beyond what I decided to put on the page as a way of explanation.

The reason people do what others tell them to turns out to be simple. In his brilliant book, *In Defense of Anarchism*, Robert Paul Wolff notes that obedience isn't simply a matter of doing what someone else tells you to do; it is "a matter of doing what he tells you to do *because he tells you to do it*" (emphasis original) (Wolff, 1998). In other words, it is because that someone is perceived of being in a position of authority that grants them the right to tell you what to do. But why follow what those in authority tell us to do? It's because adherence to the demands of authority feels like it provides a foundation of security in life and relief from the uncertainty continually shaping human experience. It allows us to stop being creative and to limit our improvisational activity (I don't think we ever entirely stop improvising) and, instead, live only guided by the riffs and licks of convention and conviction often established by those in power. Our willingness to toe the line has benefits in that it allows us to maintain social order and, through that, live largely as we wish as long as we have the economic wherewithal to do so. But this willingness also allows people to easily follow ideologies that promise to give them what they want and is an important reason why humans continue to lean in the direction of fascist or authoritarian cultural lead sheets associated with perspectives like Trumpism, Chinese Communism, or Naziism. MAGA promised security and certainty by returning America to an imagined authentic past in which life was better, at least for straight white people, and in which things didn't appear to change much and those who wish for that past felt free to openly voice their dislike for anyone unlike themselves. That past, of course, is an illusion. It never existed, even for the white people who want it to return. But as an idealized Rockwellian illustration, the MAGA lead sheet works because it taps into the human tendency to categorize the world in terms of binaries—in this case, the binaries of past and present, Black and White, secure and insecure, us and them, which are then symbolically transmuted into the binary of good and evil as leaders like Trump improvise on the social riffs and licks of their political ideology.

I happen to agree with much of what Bernie Sanders proposes in terms of the direction the US should move in the future as well as much of what the Biden Administration is proposing for a social and economic overhaul of American society. I think democratic socialism is a reasonable political and economic approach that limits the disregard for human suffering that so often accompanies the unbridled capitalism associated with the sentiments of groups like Trumpsters. But I also recognize that it has a way of setting up the same types of binaries that MAGA does. Those on the far Left have a similar tendency to categorize the world in terms of Us vs. Them, which becomes a way to symbolically represent good and evil and situate oneself unambiguously on the side of good. In both far left and far right political perspectives—and even within the middle—people align themselves with their leaders and do what their leaders ask of them, because they see it as being in their self-interest, which is constructed in terms of freedom from uncertainty and insecurity. Politicians don't really offer social programs or tax cuts to make people's lives better; they offer feelings of security and release from uncertainty. Social programs are designed to give people financial security, as are tax cuts, by making life more financially or socially predictable. And in both approaches, what is being offered is an illusion, because freedom from insecurity only comes from embracing it. It arises from embracing the idea that one's convictions are potentially wrong and recognizing that in a world of constant change there is no certainty to be had.

Religious faith can operate in the same way. To claim a position of unwavering faith in a religious doctrine or a particular deity is to situate one's identity in a place that attempts to limit or even eliminate uncertainty. In 2012, the Republican Party of Texas approved a political platform for the midterm election campaign that took an interesting approach to education. The platform stated, "We oppose the teaching of Higher Order Thinking Skills (HOTS) (values clarification), critical thinking skills and similar programs that...have the purpose of challenging the student's fixed beliefs..." This position from America's evangelical right wing is unsurprising but, I think, reflects the mindsets of many people from all sides of the political spectrum who do not want to have their fixed beliefs challenged by opposing perspectives that question the authority and authenticity of their own ideas about values such as justice and faith. The problem with critical thinking, as presented above, is that it undermines certainty, which leads to insecurity about one's own moral, political, and philosophical judgments. I see this as a positive, not a negative, because critical thinking undermines the illusion of certainty which, in turn, leads to intellectual humility.

As noted earlier, I am not arguing for a middle path; I am arguing that we need to abandon unwavering *conviction* about our beliefs. This is difficult for Americans and many others who adhere to absolutist tropes about politics, religion and ethics because we are told virtually from birth that we should follow our beliefs and fight for our convictions. We are told to have the courage to stay true to our convictions and have the courage to do what we think is right. There are plenty of websites out there, particularly religious ones, that tell us it is important to live our convictions and, as one Christian site aimed at women puts it,[11] "convictions set us apart from animals and play a fundamental role in molding our character." The author of the page goes on to note how difficult it is to keep to one's Christian convictions in a world that seems to be so lacking in them.

This type of thinking is dualistic—it is the us and them way of organizing the world—and this kind of deep adherence to one's convictions usually is a product of a binary mindset that sees certainty as good and uncertainty as bad. It's also

---

11   https://www.projectinspired.com/how-to-stay-true-to-your-convictions/

an arrogant way of putting the world together that leaves little space for alternate perspectives and different sensibilities. Interestingly, in the above quotation, the binaries are found not only in the juxtaposition between Christians and non-Christians (who lack Christian convictions) but between humans and other animals, who lack the ability even to have the convictions to which humans often so rigidly adhere. I'm not sure how they know what non-human animals are thinking, but I think one of my dogs has pretty strong convictions about her love for my daughter. She also has, perhaps, even stronger convictions about the joys of food. Of course, these are unlikely to be ideological, philosophical, or religious convictions, but they are commitments that involve feelings of selfless love and loyalty, commitments expressed not only by humans but by many other animals.

In 2008, the Academy Award for the best foreign language film went to a Japanese movie called *Okuribito* or *Departures* in English. The film is a touching exploration of the struggle a young man experiences as he gives up his career as a cellist to return to his natal home with his wife, who willingly joins him in their new life. Needing to find employment, Daigo, the protagonist, finds a position as an undertaker's assistant. It's a good job but given the taboo on occupations related to death that has existed in Japan for centuries, the work is not viewed positively by others in the town. Uncomfortable with the potential social stigma and perhaps initially somewhat embarrassed by the work, Daigo tries to keep his new position secret from his wife. Of course, she eventually learns about how he has been making money and walks out on him as a result of both his deception and her discomfort with the kind of work her husband has been doing to make ends meet. She seems rather selfish to the viewer, a point that is confirmed when she returns to Daigo after learning she is pregnant. When she reappears in Daigo's life, she asks him to resign from the undertaker position, but Daigo refuses. He has become committed to what he is doing and, in fact, has found a way, through caring for the deceased, to care for the living. He pursues his work with humble sincerity and quality. When the owner of the local bath house dies, Daigo's wife follows her husband to the private preparation of the corpse and is overcome by the delicacy, warmth, and kindness with which he prepares the body for cremation and by the value of his compassionate work for the loved ones left behind. She sees that what her husband does is meaningful and that in his work there is an identification between himself and the deceased through which the entire family is able to express and experience the moment as one of both suffering and quiescent acceptance. I don't usually cry at movies, but this scene gets me every time I watch it. It is a powerful expression of undifferentiated love.

Throughout the story, we learn that Daigo has deeply negative feelings toward his father, who left him as a child and the movie reaches its climax when Daigo learns that his father has died. At first, he refuses to travel to the town where his father's corpse is located and resists becoming involved in managing his father's final affairs, but eventually, at the urging of a colleague who left her child as a little boy, decides to go to prepare his father's body. In the case of both Daigo and his wife, as well as other characters in the film, the story revolves around overcoming selfish desires grounded in certainty about the truth of pre-established cultural scripts such as the stigmatization of corpses. Each of the characters finds a way to adjust to the needs of others by releasing their sense of certainty about life and the future. Daigo's commitment to the cello is shattered by his inability to find work as a cellist and he is forced to follow a different, and rather uncertain, path that unfolds in a difficult direction. But he lets the kaleidoscope turn and finds a new direction in life as a mortician where he can express the same kind of concern and quality he did as a cellist.

Daigo and his wife come to the realization that that neither of them is an autonomous being able to simply do those things they wish to do. They live in a community of people who need and rely upon each other, and as Daigo's wife comes to realize the importance of his work to that community, a sense of differentiation between the couple feels as though it begins to dissolve, particularly when Daigo, himself, faces his own self-centered attitudes and anger about his father. What is so striking to me in this film is that in each case the overcoming of selfishness lies in the capacity to sympathize and attempt to empathize with another and to see the beauty of that other's life and actions, even when one has been angry about the ways in which the other has behaved. The film captures the sense in Japanese ideas about the world that the moral good arises in beauty and beauty arises in the identification of self and other.[12]

The notion of the moral self as an autonomous entity is a common trope in Western philosophical literature. It can be found in the writings of Locke, Mill, Kant, Kierkegaard, Nietzsche, Hare, and many others, and is typically seen by ethicists like my professor at the University of Virginia as being central to the preservation of liberty and rights and freedom from those who would interfere with our ability to function as independent moral beings.

Zen is a philosophy that shows us a way in which, rather than the separating tendencies of a philosophy of human-autonomy-as-isolation, a sense of self and other grounded in the realization that, although we cannot fully empathize with any other being, we can experience life through the fact that we are all expressions of being itself. This opens the possibility for a society less structured around binaries of good and evil, right and wrong, and opens us to the possibility of pursuing life around Quality expressed in the concern for the needs of others, even if that means not always having things exactly as we might want them to be or completely grasping what motivates those needs that others display. For Japanese, I think, and at least to a degree drawing on the philosophy of Zen, there is a sense that the path to undifferentiation is found in lived awareness that humans exist embedded in social context and that individual autonomy unrestricted by the value of identification

---

12   This scenes is also discussed in my book *Rethinking Autonomy* (2013).

dehumanizes by setting people into simple binaries grounded in unwavering conviction about the truth of the beliefs held by the groups associated with those binaries.

To move in this direction means to recognize that the collective improvisation of our social reality implies that humans are not the product of creation. They are the agents of creation. This was, I believe, the point Rorty was making in that article on post-modern bourgeois liberalism that had such a profound impact on my own thinking. Rorty was pushing us to understand that conversations about ethics need to move away from discussions of right or wrong as grounded in a reality external to our own experience of the world and the need to identify an *a priori* reality that can infuse certainty into our thoughts about how to live and behave as moral creatures. Instead, it would be better for us to accept uncertainty and change, which would lead us to build moralities, plural, that reflect the contingent nature of our understanding both about the world and ourselves. To accept contingency is to take a position of epistemological humility in which we avoid perspectives that convey absolute conviction to any position. Proximate conviction certainly makes sense; I have a basic belief that the position of democratic socialism works better than unbridled capitalism that is based on my own experiences traveling to societies that are organized around democratic socialist principles. I think they are considerably more humane than what I see in the United States. But I also want to stay open to the ideas of free-market capitalists who also have a perspective that makes sense to them, and probably know something about the world that would help to make some form of democratic socialism work in American society if the opportunity were to arise for that particular ideology to take significant hold in the American imagination.

I remain agnostic about the "truth" of democratic socialism, just as I do about the indecency of unbridled capitalism. Empirically, based on my own observations of the world and my reading of history, I think an unrestricted capitalist society is likely to harm many and benefit a few, while a democratic socialist society is more likely to benefit many, while harming a few. But there is a discussion to be had about which perspective might work best in the America of 2021 or about what innovative improvisation upon both systems might be developed to address the needs of our society at this particular historical moment. But we must talk to each other and accept, on all sides, that there is an inherent uncertainty about how any approach might work out in the long run because humans can't predict the future.

Humans in all cultures share the experience of emotions and the ability to create rational ways of responding to the world, but the manner in which these are formed, expressed, and interpreted depends on localized experience and the varied lead sheets people use to navigate their world. Right and wrong are not objective values evident in an objective reality to which we have access and that can be discovered through careful exploration of our own intuitions. Right and wrong, good and evil, are products of human invention and creativity. They are currents of improvisation that move and shift as people improvise new and novel ways of being in the world. This is why I find the cancel culture of the 2020s problematic, even if I agree with many of the perspectives expressed among those engaged in cancelling—it's an attempt to say that there is only one truth that is completely removed from the currents and flows of historical and cultural context. It's an ahistorical, acultural take on the world that seeks to extinguish those attitudes and behaviors many, at this moment in that flow, have deemed wrong. It sets up the world in binaries of right and wrong and situates individuals in terms of their convictions without giving much thought to how those convictions and ideas emerged in the heads of the wrong-behaving other.

The point I want to leave with the reader is that morality is a creative process—humans invent right and wrong in different ways depending upon social context, history, and perceptions about human needs. Ethics are a product of improvisation and improvisation is something we typically do in groups. But improvisation inherently generates uncertainty. I never know exactly where the music will go when my trio is performing, and I never even know exactly where my solos will go. If I only played the licks in my solos, they would become very boring very quickly, not only to my audiences but also to me. If we were to view our lives, including our moral lives, as creative processes co-constructed in the flow of social improvisation, we might be more able to embrace the uncertainty with which that flow unfolds. And, as I have tried to show throughout this book, to embrace uncertainty is to release commitment to absolutes and with it to diminish the suffering that comes from clinging to desires that may never be captured and changes in the flow of life that never resolve.

FURTHER READING

Abe, Masao. (2003). *Zen and the Modern World: A Third Sequel to Zen and Western Thought.* University of Hawai'i Press.

Buber, Martin. (2012). *I and Thou.* eBookit.com.

Carlson, Kyogen. (1994). *Zen in the American Grain: Discovering the Teachings at Home.* Station Hill Press.

Coupey, Phillippe. (1995). *Sit: Zen Teachings of Master Taisen Deshimaru.* Hohm Press.

Dawkins, Richard. (2008). *The God Delusion.* Mariner Books.

_____. (2015). *The Blind Watchmaker: Why the Evidence of Evolution Reveals a Universe without Design.* W. W. Norton & Co.

Feynman, Richard. (2005). *The Meaning of It All: Thoughts of a Citizen Scientist.* Basic Books.

Firestein, Steven. (2012). *Ignorance: How It Drives Science.* Oxford University Press.

Fox, Douglas A. (1968). Soteriology in Jodo Shin and Christianity. *Contemporary Religions in Japan*, 9(1/2), 30–51.

Gay, David. (2000). Moral Boundaries and Deviant Music: Public Attitudes toward Heavy Metal and Rap. *Deviant Behavior*, 21(1), 63–85.

Geertz, Clifford. (1957). Ritual and Social Change: A Javanese Example. *American Anthropologist*, 59(1), 32–54.

_____. (1985). *Local Knowledge: Further Essays in Interpretive Anthropology.* Basic Books.

Haviland, William A. (2005). *Cultural Anthropology: The Human Challenge.* 11th ed. Thomson Wadsworth.

Herrigel, Eugen. (1989). *Zen in the Art of Archery.* Vintage Books.

Hershorn, Tad. (2011). *Norman Granz: The Man Who Used Jazz for Justice.* University of California Press.

Ivanhoe, Philip J. (2017). *Oneness: East Asian Conceptions of Virtue, Happiness, and How We are All Connected.* Oxford University Press.

Jenkins, Sarah (ed). (1999). *Buddha Facing the Wall: Interviews with American Zen Monks.* Present Perfect Books.

Kaag, John. (2016). *American Philosophy: A Love Story.* Farrar, Straus and Giroux.

_____. (2018). *Hiking with Nietzsche: On Becoming Who You Are.* Farrar, Straus and Giroux.

Kelly, Robin. (2010). *Thelonious Monk: The Life and Times of an American Original.* Free Press.

Keddy, Paul A. (2020). *Darwin Meets the Buddha: Human Nature, Buddha Nature, Wild Nature.* Sumeru Books.

Kraft, Kenneth. (2018). *Zen Traces: Exploring American Zen with Twain and Thoreau.* Paul Dry Books.

LaFleur, William. (ed). (1985). *Dogen Studies.* University of Hawaii Press.

Lebra, Takie. (1976). *Japanese Patterns of Behavior.* University of Hawaii Press.

Lee, Edward Ashford. (2020). *The Coevolution: The Entwined Futures of Humans and Machines.* MIT Press.

Margenau, Henry. (1964). *Ethics & Science.* Van Nostrand.

_____. (1977). *The Nature of Physical Reality: A Philosophy of Modern Physics.* Ox Bow Press.

_____. (1984). The Miracle of Existence. Ox Bow Press.

McDaniel, Richard Bryan. (2015). *Cypress Trees in the Garden: The Second Generation of Zen Teaching in America.* Sumeru Books.

Nisensen, Eric. (2001). *The Making of Kind of Blue.* St. Martin's Press.

Nishitani, Keiji. (1990). *The Self-Overcoming of Nihilism*. State University of New York Press.

Pirsig, Robert. (1974). *Zen and the Art of Motorcycle Maintenance*. William Morrow and Company.

Rorty, Richard. (1980). *Philosophy and the Mirror of Nature*. Blackwell.

_____. (1983). Postmodernist Bourgeois Liberalism. *The Journal of Philosophy*, 80(10), 583–589.

_____. (1989). *Contingency, Irony, and Solidarity*. Cambridge University Press.

Sauer, Glenn. 2020. *Points of Contact: Science, Religion, and the Search for Truth*. Orbis.

Schrödinger, Erwin. (2008). *My View of the World*. Cambridge University Press.

Stevens, John. (2007). *Zen Bow, Zen Arrow: The Life and Teachings of Awa Kenzo, the Archery Master from Zen in the Art of Archery*. Shambhala.

Tam, Shek-Wing. (2019). *Fourfold Dependent Arising and the Profound Prajnaparamita*. Sumeru Books.

Tillich, Paul. (1963). *The Eternal Now*. Scribner.

Traphagan, John W. (2004). *The Practice of Concern: Ritual, Well-being, and Aging in Rural Japan*. Carolina Academic Press.

_____. (2008). Embodiment, Ritual Incorporation, and Cannibalism among the Iroquoians after 1300 CE. *Journal of Ritual Studies*, 22(2): 1-12.

_____. (2013). *Rethinking Autonomy: A Critique of Principlism in Biomedical Ethics*. SUNY Press.

_____. (2019). Cargoism and Scientific Justification in the Search for Extraterrestrial Intelligence. *Zygon: Journal of Religion and Science*, 54(1), 29–45.

_____. (2020). *Cosmopolitan Rurality, Depopulation, and Entrepreneurial Ecosystems in 21st Century Japan*. Cambria Press.

Vertesi, Janet. (2020). *Shaping Science: Organizations, Decisions, and Culture on NASA's Teams*. University of

Chicago Press.

Watts, Alan. (1975). *Tao: The Watercourse Way*. Pantheon.

_____. (2000). *What is Zen?* New World Library.

_____. (2011). *The Wisdom of Insecurity*. Knopf Doubleday Publishing Group.

Wexler, Bruce. (2006). *Brain and Culture: Neurobiology, Ideology, and Social Change*. MIT Press.

Wolff, Robert Paul. (1998). *In Defense of Anarchism*. University of California Press.

Wong, David. (1984). *Moral Relativity*. University of California Press.

Yamada, Shoji. (2011). *Shots in the Dark: Japan, Zen, and the West*. University of Chicago Press.

Yokoi, Yūho. (1976). *Zen Master Dogen: An Introduction with Selected Writings*. Weatherhill.